WALKING
DOWN
A DREAM

To Rosemary,
lots of love
Natasha

WALKING
DOWN
A DREAM

Mexico to Canada on Foot

Natasha Carver

To order additional copies of this book, contact:
Xlibris Corporation
1-888-795-4274
www.Xlibris.com
Orders@Xlibris.com
16547

CONTENTS

AFTER

ACKNOWLEDGEMENTS

Trek 2000 was undertaken in order to raise money for sustainability projects in Bolivia and Peru through Oxfam. The total raised was £12,039 (approximately US$18,000). I would like to thank everyone who helped us to raise this amount, most particularly our patron Lord Montgomery, Jonny Tarling, and my mother.

With huge thanks to all Trail Angels and special thanks to:

Wayne and Janet, Jeff, Donna, the water lady, Richard at W-W Ranch, Paul at Anza, Meadow Ed, Helen and Don Middleton, Ben and Anna Marie, Charles, Jack Fair, Adrianna, Lily and Larry, Andy and Mike at Crabtree Meadows, the ex-Scouts by Lake Marjorie, Rich, Bill and Molly, Norman, Robin Brierley, Andy at Drakesbad, Jehovah's Witnesses at Old Station, the fire-fighter at the caves, Brenda and Diane, Floyd, Eric and Donavan, George, King County Search and Rescue Team, and all the people who gave me lifts, sent me packages, and fed and watered me.

With thanks to all my fellow hikers for their energy, their stories, and for being there:

Kris, Purple and Oasis, Bald Eagle and Nocona, Bluefoot, Amigo, Tripod and Dawn, Falling Water and Drip, Beaker, the Lonely Wolf, John, Mike, Darris, Kirk, Doc Rudy, Mudflap, Charlie and Lady Godiva, Mike, Janet, Christopher, Max and Robyn, Matt, Flatfoot, Itchy, Scratchy and Captain America, Hobbit, Staggering Willy and the Menacing Vegetables, Seth and Rick, Hawkeye and Tweedle, Hamsa and John, Willy Color,

Blisterfree, Woody, Sparrow Hawk and Terry, the Jesus Freaks, Scott Yo-yo Williamson, Madam Butterfly and Improv, Rise and Shine, Steve and Celest, Let-it-be, Turtle and Lora, and most especially the Wolfpack: Vive, Glen, Wonder, Kadiddle and Wonderwoman.

With grateful thanks to all the book angels:

Nick, Matt, Mandy, Peter, David, Antonia.

Thank you to Nick Bowyer for his drawing, Gentle Ben Go and the PCTA for permission to reprint the graph of Southern California taken from the *Pacific Crest Trail Data Book*, Wilderness Press for permission to quote from the two volumes of *The Pacific Crest Trail Guide Book,* and Ray Jardine for permission to quote from *The Pacific Crest Trail Hiker's Handbook*. Every attempt has been made to contact Jim Podlesney.

How can a book describe the psychological factors a person must prepare for . . . the despair, the alienation, the anxiety, and especially the pain, both physical and mental, which slices to the very heart of the hiker's volition, which are the real things that must be planned for?

Jim Podlesney, *Pacific Crest Trail Hike Planning Guide*

Strange the faithless fuss made about taking a walk in the safest and pleasantest of all places, a wilderness.

John Muir

BEFORE

PREPARATION

"I'm an actress."

"Oh, really?"

Obviously it was the wrong answer.

"I . . . I work as an actress," I corrected, trying to sound convincing, "Theatre in Education, actually. I'm a teacher."

Now he looked almost bored. Let me into your goddamn country, I glared back at him through my forced smile. He flicked through my passport.

"Is that what you were doing in Bolivia? Where you met this 'Canadian friend'?"

He made it sound as if she were make-believe.

"Yes, we were both teaching," I said, realising too late that the Bolivian Visa stated in big black letters *no puede trabajar* (not permitted to work). "We met in Bolivia and now we're walking 2600 miles to raise money for the people there."

It sounded totally implausible, even to me.

"In Canada?"

"No, from Mexico to Canada." It was about the third time I'd told him. "I only want to stay here for three days, then I'm going to the States."

"How much money have you got?"

I looked in my purse, still not thinking straight.

"Um, ten pounds."

"Ten pounds?" He asked incredulously.

"Oh, well, I've got a visa card. And I've got 1000 pounds worth of Canadian dollars traveller's cheques," I remembered, which I did have, to pay back Kris, my 'Canadian friend', for the gear and food she'd bought for both of us for the trek. He counted through the cheques, went away, made me wait. There were glass walls to the unnamed people-who-can't-just-be-let-in section. In the booth next to me a Japanese guy was receiving the same treatment from a woman who kept peering at him over the top of her glasses. He needed a translator. This is ridiculous, I thought, I'm British, it's not meant to be a problem for a British citizen to enter a Commonwealth country like Canada—don't they even like the Queen more than we do? My official returned.

"So, you've got 1000 pounds of Canadian dollars traveller's cheques and you're staying three days."

It wasn't really a question. It was a statement of disbelief.

"I need to buy a lot of equipment. We're walking 2600 miles," I repeated.

It was too ridiculous not to be true, and eventually he let me through. I came out of the airport to greet Kris, the Canadian friend I hadn't seen for two years.

I am/was/have been an actress. Of sorts. What I've really been doing is running round audiences of screaming Spanish six-year-olds being followed pantomime-style by an unconvincing monster whilst trying to hold on to a pair of orange flares that have a faulty zip and not lose my shiny silver wig to the more criminally-minded of the kids. Don't ask me how this teaches them any English. I've performed in gyms, aircraft hangers, state-of-the-art theatres, cinemas and school halls. I've been chased out of a hostel down the street by a mad woman covered in white powder and red lipstick screaming "Why? Why?" at me, plagued for kisses by packs of pre-pubescent Spaniards, pretended to be a pilgrim in Galicia, and tried to explain in Spanish to teachers, the deep moral core of a play for 17-year-olds which celebrates teenage drinking and sex. And through it all pleaded with my shady boss, who is like Colombo on a bad day, working for the other side, to (a) not call me 'lovely'— I have a name; it's Natasha—and (b) pay me. At the time of writing this, I've given up on the first, and am still, perhaps naively, waiting for the second.

And why did I subject myself to this? Because I need money. I need about 3000 pounds in order to finance the walk from Mexico to Canada along the Pacific Crest Trail—a wilderness route through California, Oregon and Washington. At this stage I don't know a lot about it. I've read the guide books. I know there are rattlesnakes, bears and mosquito-infested forests. I know water, or lack of it, is a problem. I've made charts on the computer: where and when to the next water source, names and places that mean nothing to me—Burnt Rancheria, Chariot Canyon, Rodriguez Spur, Scissors Crossing, Apache Springs. I know the mileage between each town and I know that if we walk 15 miles a day with one day off every two weeks, we will arrive in Canada in approximately 175 days, which is six months. My friend and hiking partner knows a lot more. She has been preparing all our food boxes which her parents will send from Canada one by one, a month before we are due to arrive at each place. Every day Kris and I send endless emails to each other. *Do you like soya nuts? To what degree should our sleeping bags be rated? How many socks are you taking? Do you think we should use trekking poles? Are you buying leather boots? What are soya nuts?*

I met Kris in Bolivia two years ago. I wanted to explore the countryside, the mountains, but didn't know how to go about it. Kris was keen on the idea and seemed to have a lot of camping experience. We bought a tent.

First it was just a day-hike, which ended with a hazardous crossing of a river that contained most of La Paz's waste. Undeterred, we moved further out for a three-day 'run' down from the altiplano to the jungle. It was so cold one night that my contact lenses froze in their salt solution. And then every weekend we were hiking, climbing mountains, exploring. I got hypothermia, Kris developed a foot problem. Our stove broke and we lived off crackers and stale bread for three days. We got lost, ran from a forest fire, and saw some of the most beautiful mountain scenery on earth. We felt indestructible and wanted more.

It was a crazy idea. 2600 miles. From Mexico to Canada. Kris told me about the trail—nice, I thought, but not necessary, and not very practical, not realistic. It was a more of a fantasy than a dream: the kind you get whilst gorging on chocolate cake and promising yourself that you'll become an athlete tomorrow. Kris went back to Canada. I went on to Ecuador, still on course for a healthy middle-class existence.

Then love (and life) fell apart.

Walking was all I could think of. At night, my feet were walking already. Any gap in conversation, any break in thought, any slight feeling of panic, inadequacy or despair and I was walking, walking. It was therapeutic. In my mind I'd walk until I was sleep-walking, walking into oblivion. Sometimes, escaping from the show of functioning in everyday life, I'd set out, half hoping to be as vigilant as at night and walk to eternity. I'd walk an hour, maybe two, out of the town, out, aiming to go straight like an arrow into the unknown. I was Jason setting off in search of the edge of the earth, Orpheus heading for the underworld. But fate, or subconscious will, took me round in a circle each time. Back on the edge of town I'd resign myself to staying around another day and walk back to the flat.

Eventually, I came back to the UK, got a job as a tour guide and dreamt about walking. Kris was working for the Canadian government. We corresponded by email.

There has to be more than this. More to life. I don't want 2.4 kids and a house in suburbia. I don't want a nine-to-five job, staring glumly past the indifferent faces on the tube every morning, or to get qualified to sit at a desk and watch a screen all day. I don't want a career that I have to stick with for fear of falling behind, or to socialise after work in chain pubs with watery beer. "Isn't it time you settled down?" people ask, that ever-so-kind way of saying "When are you going to start paying taxes for all that education you had?" It's two years since I left university, seven years since I left school. This is no longer a 'having fun before . . . ' time, this is my life.

"Let's go," I said to Kris.

"Let's go," she said to me.

The night before the flight to Canada I am still not excited. I am frantic. I am desperately racking my brain for anything essential that I might have forgotten, left behind, something crucial that might mean we can't walk. I get out of bed and double check my passport and visa for the umpteenth time. What else have I forgotten to do? I have a nightmare: Kris has broken her leg but she has been too scared to tell me, knowing how disappointed I will be. When I arrive at the airport she is in plaster, crying, on crutches. This can't be true. Nothing can prevent this hike from happening.

I say goodbye to my family at the airport, still convinced that my dream is true and I'll be back home in a week or so. I am nervous, my father is resigned, my sister is excited, my mother says;

"I think this is the most ridiculous idea you've ever had."

In Vancouver it's raining. We're talking so much as we leave the airport that we end up lost inside some car park complex. Even the rain feels good. We're walking from Mexico to Canada. Kris is bright-eyed, sparky. We take one bus, then another through what seems like endless miles of city sprawl. Soon I will be out of all this, out of the pollution, out of the grey. Soon our only concerns will be pack weight and water. Life will be simple. Noise will be crickets and birds. Peace. That is what I'm looking for, that is what I'm expecting. A very self-satisfying peace of climbing up to a pass, looking around, feeling on top of the world. There will be endless miles of trail stretching out before us. My body is ready for the physical challenge. It wants to walk walk walk. It can scarcely wait to begin, to be off these hard pavements and on to a dusty track. My muscles are itching to go.

Really it's running away. I'm running away from love. Or the lack of it. I would like to reach a point where I need no-one and no-one needs me. To become perfectly independent, serenely self-sufficient. I will subsist. I want to walk until I forget. Walk until there is nothing that matters but walking. I know there will be physical pain and I know it will (should) be a pain I can tolerate, but enough for it to empty my mind. I will walk my emotions into control, drill my soul with self-reliance. Mexico to Canada.

Kris is bubbly and vivacious, she giggles at anything. Each time I catch her eyes on the bus she grins widely and shouts things above the traffic noise. She has always been enthusiastic and her emails have been full of 'We're going to do it!'

I know we're going to do it. It doesn't feel like arrogance, I just feel a quiet confidence of determination. I know we will get to Canada, simply because we can.

People ask questions like, "Do you think you'll get along?" Six months, 24 hours a day. Difficulties are inevitable. I remember Kris talked all the time. Will this drive me mad? How will I annoy her? Too indecisive? Too forthright? I've pictured us laughing. We will make it.

The two days in Vancouver pass in a flurry of buying last-minute things. Kris is stressed. She has done an incredible amount of work towards this hike. All the food boxes are packed neatly with the address to each post office stuck on to each one. *'Please hold for PCT hikers'*, they say, *'Expected Date of Arrival: . . . '* Kris has dried large amounts of fruit and vegetables in her dehydrator. In each box we get at least one packet of dried fruit for every day. She has weighed out nuts and seeds into separate bags. There are soya nuts, pumpkin seeds, almonds, corn nuts, sunflower seeds, peanuts, and walnuts. They are salted, unsalted, roasted, and in spicy sauce. Variety is going to be essential if we are to carry on eating this for six months. Then there is a shocking amount of pasta or rice for each meal and dried spaghetti sauce to go with it. Kris is vegetarian and it is very important to make sure we get enough protein and vitamins. Everything has been calculated by calories, weight and fuel (i.e. energy giving potential). She sent over small samples of things like dehydrated black bean sauce, which dries out as dark brown crumbly rocks, that must have looked very suspicious to customs officials. I was meant to have tasted them, but instead I used them to shock and enthral people into donating money. "We're going to live off this!" I would say, producing some miniature grey trees that were once broccoli, without ever really stopping to think that it was true, that I was going to live off these unidentifiable dried pieces of vegetation for the next six months. That and peanut butter.

We have packed our 'drift box' which we will send from post office to post office with any extras we think we might need—aloe vera for sunburn, bandages, tampons, films, plasters, duct tape, pens and paper, along with many ridiculous things that we will never use, and batteries, batteries by the zillions. We're leaving at 4.30 a.m. By midnight I am packed. Or not.

"Kris!" I wail, "I can't fit everything in."

Kris is fixed to her laptop in a grey haze. She looks vaguely up at me.

"Yes you can. Unpack and start again."

I try again. This time with a bit more success.

We have with us:

- Two backpacks (weighing approximately five pounds each which is too much, but they are comfortable)
- Two synthetic sleeping bags rated to minus seven
- Two silk liners
- Two ultralite thermarest sleeping mats which are self-inflating
- Water filter
- Two four-litre water bags and drinking hoses
- Four two-litre water bags (total capacity = eight litres per person)
- Multifuel camp stove and fuel bottle
- Pot and handle
- Food bag and cord for hanging
- Tarp and building wrap for a groundsheet
- Watch
- Two cameras
- Two penknives
- Two head-torches
- Two flashlights
- First aid kit
- Fire starting kit + birthday candles
- Mylar blanket
- Two Gore-Tex jackets
- Two mosquito shirts
- Two fleeces
- Two thermal tops
- Two sarongs

- Two wool hats
- Six pairs of socks
- Two pairs of plastic sandals/aqua socks for river crossings
- Toothpaste
- Two toothbrushes
- Moisturiser
- Aloe vera
- Deodorant
- Vaseline

I am wearing: leather boots, thin cotton zip-off trousers, a sports-bra, a pink cotton vest top, and a white T-shirt. Kris has: sneakers, shorts, a sports-bra, and a thin white shirt.

We also have:

- One two-person North Face tent
- Two pairs of instep crampons
- Two ice-axes
- Two pairs of quick-drying trousers
- Two pairs of gloves

These things have been sent to Onyx and Kennedy Meadows, the start of the Sierras where we are expecting snow.

Eventually I sleep. Kris continues on her laptop, hastily ramming everything into her pack just as we are about to leave. And then it's through the grey darkness to Seattle airport from where we will fly to San Diego. Nothing seems quite real. I suddenly feel awfully old to be starting off on such an adventure. Am I wasting my life? What am I doing here? I've had my fun already. I've 'found myself', taken time out, had a gap year, actually three of them. Is this selfish? Is it Saturday? I should be shopping or something, shouldn't I? But then I remember, I hate shopping. I'm not that keen on London. I don't even really like going out that much. This is me. I'm walking from Mexico to Canada. That's definitely me. 2600 miles.

Natasha and Kris

SOUTHERN CALIFORNIA

SEND-OFF

There's a guy called Jeff meeting us. Kris found him on the Internet. This isn't as careless as it sounds—the Pacific Crest Trail (PCT) has an association and a web site. There's a chat-room with endless pages of agonising over feet and footwear. There are T-shirts, maps, the guide books and news of trail maintenance. Jeff has offered to take us from San Diego airport to Lake Morena Campground near the border where a 'send-off' party will be held for this year's hikers. Jeff is our first Trail Angel—someone who gives up their time to help hikers.

By the time we arrive at the campground it's dark and we stumble towards the glow of a fire and the group of older, larger, grey-haired Californians.

"Hikers!" someone says, and a hushed awe falls on the party. I am confused and very tired. Who are all these people? Kris and I fumble around in the dark struggling with our new tarp. 'Tarp' is a fancy name for a sheet of green plastic. With a certain amount of practice and skill it can be strung up, even without trees, to form a roof. We have a piece of building wrap instead of a ground sheet. Jeff quizzed us on arrival:

"Are you tarping or tenting it?"

"Tarp," we said.

"Yes!" he shouted, as though his favourite team had scored a goal.

I have never seen a tarp before. Kris has used this one, but only with trees.

I read two books before setting off. One by a woman called Cindy and the other by the legendary Ray Jardine. About the former I remember two things: she found it hard to walk with people day in day out; and there was a terrifying account of a fall down a steep snowfield. Ray Jardine wrote the *Pacific Crest Trail*

Handbook[1] and is, I am realising rapidly, something of a guru for hikers. I've heard his name mentioned more times in the last twenty-four hours than I have the words 'Pacific Crest Trail'. I read the extracts from his book that Kris highlighted for me on the plane on the way over. He advocates carrying an umbrella and wearing running shoes amongst other ideas. He doesn't quite go so far as to advise you to cut off the end of your toothbrush, but many people here at the campground have. Dissatisfied with many commercial products, Ray Jardine began making much of his own equipment, the designs of which are now sold under the 'GoLite' brand name. The Jardine way is the new way of hiking. Instead of the Scout philosophy of 'Be Prepared', which means you carry the kitchen sink in case of any eventualities, Ray says 'Go Light!' unto his hikers, or words to that effect. The message is to carry only the bare necessities. His pack weighs a mere nine pounds without food and water. Kris is very keen, she has gone with the gym shoes, but I've managed to talk her out of umbrellas. (An umbrella? In the wilderness? Allow me some street cred, please . . . .) Our packs weigh around 30 pounds each, without food and water.

Hence, thanks to Mr. Jardine, the tarp. It's a good deal lighter than a tent and, apparently, better in the rain due to the fact that it is open at either end and therefore gathers less condensation. I am sceptical. It's seven o'clock when I crawl out of my sleeping bag and ease myself around the hiking pole. The non-hikers have been up since five in the morning and a group of them are now surrounding our sagging piece of plastic.

"Hi," I blink, still on my elbows.

They nod a greeting and send out embarrassed mutters to each other as they turn away. Our tarp, it seems, is the wrong way up.

And how exactly *can* a green plastic sheet be the wrong way up? Well, that takes a true 'go-lighter' to know. By the time Kris crawls out of bed at lunchtime the group has already decided we're not going to make it. A couple laden with 40 pounds a piece of excess body weight, on the other hand, are odds-on favourites.

Aside of the betting on who is and who isn't going to get to Canada, the other highlight of the send-off is the gear competition.

People are lined up behind their designer creations. As the tarp is now fairly well established, the big challenge this year is between stoves. A bulky six-foot guy turns to the lean hiker standing beside him.

"*Mine's smaller than yours!*" he sings.

"Yes, well, *mine* only weighs *three ounces!*" replies the other smugly.

Each stove is tested to see how long it takes to boil a cup or two of water. The judges decide who wins with regard to weight, size, and ability to heat . . . . Ray Jardine's book has started a wave of home-made packs, stoves, torches, you name it, and they all weigh less than anything available in a shop. People show off their creations with pride—a pack weighing less than a pound (two thin straps and some mesh) wins the pack competition. There are people who have made their own of everything, people who know an awful lot and given the chance will talk about it for days.

"I found when I walked XX Trail that XXX stove/tent/boots/water filter was perfect!"

I smile fixedly and explain that I've never hiked for more than a few days before; never used a water filter, never really used a stove, am not well acquainted with any type of tent and really know next to nothing about camping. That silences each and every one of them. The odds lengthen for Kris and me. I move over to the 'veggie table'.

"Hey, Oasis!" says the girl standing next to me.

It's dark now and I look around somewhat dubiously for a watering hole. Instead there is a guy behind me who nods and says, "Purple."

I look back again. They're waiting for me to say something. It must be some kind of American game with strange rules. Do I venture a colour? Orange perhaps? Or a flower maybe?

"I'm from Britain," I say by way of explanation. "My name's Natasha."

"Purple and Oasis," says the guy again. "We're getting married along the trail at Idyllwild."

"Congratulations!" says another hiker joining the group, "Bald Eagle."

"Nocona," chips in the girl next to him.

Purple and Oasis, Bald Eagle and Nocona, Bluefoot, Amigo, Tripod and Dawn, Hollywood and Star, Kadiddle, the Lonely Wolf,

and my favourite, a father and son team called Falling Water and
Drip. It's an 'AT-thing'. There are those who have and those who
haven't walked the Appalachian Trail (and those who have, have already
been named). The AT, attempted most famously by Bill Bryson, sees
2500-3000 people at its trailhead each year. It's shorter than the
PCT, more physically demanding, but less remote and has shelters
along the way. A mere 250-odd hikers will start the PCT this year
during the months of April and May. Last year around 30 made it to
Canada. The year before, only nine arrived at the border. Some are on
an ambitious four-month plan, most are hoping for a five-month
plan and a few are doing crazy things like a three-month or six-month
trip. Leave any earlier and you have to hike through snow left from
the previous year in the Sierras; leave any later and temperatures soar
down south. The race is to get to Washington before the winter comes.
Our schedule of 15 miles a day (+ a bit more in Oregon) has us there
on the 31st October. "Too late," says everyone, "way too late."

"Oregon is flat," says Kris knowledgeably. "We'll make up the
miles in Oregon."

A few of the meat-eaters drifted over to the renegade crowd.
For 'vegetarian' you can substitute 'hippie', 'drop-out', or 'welfare
kid' in many a southerner's mind. For an ordinary American telling
the difference between a hiker and a hippie can be quite a challenge
anyway. Purple did indeed have purple hair.

"No vegetarian has ever made it," announced a Santa Claus
look-a-like, shaking his head ruefully. "One got to the Sierras once,
and then consumed three steaks in a row," he paused to take a
vicious chunk out of his hot dog, "been a vegetarian for nigh on 15
years too."

Kris was not interested in rising to the challenge. She did not
really seem interested in rising to any challenge and was still in the
same zombied fog in which she had left Canada. Just tired, I
thought. Tired and stressed after all the preparation she had done.

"We're eating a lot of nuts and seeds," I volunteered.

Santa Claus raised his eyebrows and gave a significant nod to
his beefy companion. We had obviously just dropped to complete
outsiders in the betting stakes.

Day 1—0 trail miles north
US/Mexican border

Donna, another Trail Angel, drove us to the border. There's a metal fence made with runway repair panels and a maze of jeep trails crawling with border control vehicles. The dust is swirling round. It feels cold and hot at the same time. Or maybe that's just me. I think my automatic thought: What have I forgotten? *Forgotten?* creaks my body in horror as it sways under the weight of the pack. I may have to start walking because I'm not sure that I can stand up for too much longer. Donna is very excited for us; she is jumping up and down. Excited is not what I feel, in fact the emotion is registering as panic. I smile for the camera and try to stand upright. The nerve has gone in one of my legs and it's shaking uncontrollably despite, or perhaps because of, the 60 pounds weight on my back. I look to Kris to feed off her usual enthusiasm; she flashes me a gleaming smile, but the fear in her eyes leaves a slightly nauseous feeling in my stomach. Oh God, what are we doing?

Natasha and Kris at the border

We signed the PCT register staggering under the weight, using our poles to prop ourselves up (I need four legs—I would fall over without them). Then we set off for Manning Park, 2658 distant miles away on the Canadian border.

The rolling hills are covered in a fine orange dust interspersed with wild sage and yucca, dotted with white popcorn flowers. It sounds pretty: fire poppy, charming century, paintbrush, Parish's tauschia. On a postcard it would look pretty; in real life it's harsh and arid and hot. The white and green border control vehicles crawl over the hills in the distance like tropical ants. The ground along the border is swept regularly to check for footprints. Further away, along the trail, there are small piles of anonymous clothing left by escaping migrants. These days it's not just Mexicans, but people from all over the world— South Americans, Russians, Chinese. They just need hiking poles and a pack, we joke, and they could walk right into the country disguised as hikers. I wander off-trail to pee and am met abruptly by a sign: '**CUIDADO!**' it says. 'Your life is in danger from the elements'. The elements pictured include fire, rattlesnakes, lightning and drowning. Drowning? Surely not. Do they really think that having got this far, the illegal immigrant will turn back because of a signpost? '**It's not worth it!**' warns the sign. Yeah right! Only 150 years ago, it was the other way round—Americans were the illegal immigrants flooding into Mexico, and Mexican troops were attempting, equally unsuccessfully, to guard the frontier. Only then the frontier was some 1700 trail miles north at the Oregon border and California and Texas were part of Mexico. (This border was agreed in 1848 with the Treaty of Guadeloupe Hidalgo following the Mexican War.)

Our plan is to do 16 miles today. Our first day. It's quite ambitious as we're both untrained and not used to walking with a pack. Kris has been cycling regularly and I, well I've run around several theatres. Ideally we would have been training for several months. Ray Jardine says to gradually start carrying more weight with you as you get fitter, increasing the amount slightly each time. Given our condition we should only be walking eight to ten miles today and tomorrow and for the next week. But the PCT does not allow you to start gradually. It's 16 miles to the first surfacing water of Hauser Creek. In a few weeks even that will be dry. And it's hot, very hot. Hauser Creek, 16 hot miles.

People have asked me about those first few miles. What did it feel like to finally start? What did you think about?

In truth I don't remember too much. I remember the border control training ground and imagining coming across some illegal immigrants. I remember the sudden shock of a delicate pink flower. I remember walking across a railway line and taking what I thought would be an arty photo of a burnt tree. Walking with poles was strange and new. I wasn't quite sure what to do with them but knew they should be helping me. I moved the right pole with the left leg and the left pole with the right leg. The ends slipped into the sand until stopped by the rubber at the bottom. If my pack was lighter, I might have felt like a swish cross-country skier zooming along the paths. If my pack was lighter, I might have felt elegant, capable.

I don't think I thought about the trip once during the day. I think that all I thought was along the lines of: 'Just keep going; one step after the other.' I had no idea then of how fast I walked, how far we had gone, the position of the sun, what I would be eating in the next break: all the things that would become the defining elements of the routine of walking day in day out.

The first few miles we walked close together, then I led, then Kris led. Kris was fitter than me and I had trouble keeping up with her. We stopped every now and then, but I don't remember talking much. Perhaps it was too hot.

Lunchtime. Lunchtime I remember. Peanut butter and crackers. Kris told me that peanut butter is hiker food—fat and protein. You can't ask for more. Crackers are lighter than bread and they last for longer. If you haven't ever tried to swallow peanut butter and crackers in 90 degrees plus with a dry mouth and without wasting precious water, then I don't advise you to try. We had this mountain of food that we were carrying and the only way to ease the pain of the burden was to eat. A lot. But it was too hot and too dry. We were not hungry. Especially not for peanut butter and crackers. Kris got out the cookies which we rationed and we settled down hidden amongst the rocks and trees to shelter from the sun. I started writing.

> *We haven't found our friendship again yet—we are still slightly polite, cautious. Kris's sentence fragments shock my British-tuned ear. Her language seems so abrupt and jarring that I keep thinking she is angry with me. By comparison she must be infuriated as I wander around the point, never quite reaching decisiveness or clarity. In a few days we will be comfortable with one another again. In a few weeks we will know everything about each other. In a few months we will be finishing each other's sentences.*

"There's a snake!" said Kris in a slightly strangled voice of controlled panic.

I stopped writing and descended from my uncomfortable rock. There was—a snake. A brilliantly striped snake. Neither of us knows a lot about snakes.

"It's very small," I ventured. "A baby snake."

And then a thought occurred to me, "Maybe there's a nest."

It was the wrong thing to say. We both instantly became aware of every crack and crevice and tree branch from where a billion other snakes might emerge. I took a step forward and the snake, on full alert, lifted its tail and rattled. There was no *sound* of rattling as such, but it was definitely *trying* to rattle. The snake was positioned alarmingly close to the cookies. And the cookies were the only food we had any inclination to eat.

"We can't leave the cookies," I said, aghast at the thought.

I crawled underneath some branches, past the snake and scrambled over the rocks to the path. There were two pictures in my head. One, of a very small snake and two large hikers looking ridiculous, and the other, of every branch and every rock dripping with thousands of black and white stripes. We don't have a lot of snakes in Britain, apart from grass snakes which definitely hatch in large quantities from a nest. They are green and harmless. This, to my inexperienced eye, has venom written all over it—why else would it be so shiny? Kris has not encountered snakes before. She does not like them.

"You'll get used to them," I said.

"I will not get used to them," she said.

I took the packs out one by one while Kris kept me informed of the position.

"It's coming your way . . . no . . . oh shit . . . no . . . round the other side of the rock . . . no . . . coming back again . . . it's coming towards me . . . it's at the cookies . . . ahhhhhh!!!"

It was Kris and a hiking pole against the snake and the cookies.

We told this story to some hikers several days later.

"We saw a snake!"

First day, snake, that's quite a good story.

"Ahh, the King Snake, they're our friends, completely harmless, you know. They imitate rattlesnakes in order to eat them."

"Oh, um, really."

Eventually, miles later, in the dark and after straying from the path, we stumbled towards Hauser Creek. I was physically exhausted and just wanted to lie down. Is that the furthest I've ever walked in one day? Wearily we unpacked. Somewhere on the 16-mile walk one of the legs to my zip-in zip-out trousers had been left behind. Oh well, one less thing to carry—shorts it is from now on. I pumped water through the filter from the meagre supply in the creek while Kris started cooking the huge volume of food that we wouldn't want to eat. There already, lying on a piece of building wrap just like ours, was a hiker called Beaker and his friend. Beaker had sprained his ankle. First day out and you sprain your ankle. That's just gutting. Unless you're one of the five to ten per cent who give up on the first day, because it was 'not as expected'. Then a sprained ankle would be a perfect excuse to face friends and family with. Beaker was not one of these people. He was unhappy.

We ate in the dark. There was a large amount leftover. Kris scraped it into a zip-lock bag.

"Can't we bury it?" I asked.

"What you pack in, you pack out," she quoted.

Kris is well trained in 'leave no trace' camping principles.

"But it's food. It's biodegradable."

"It has all sorts of things in it that don't belong here. Seeds could sprout and ruin the natural vegetation."

She has a point. Gorse bushes brought from Scotland are causing havoc in New Zealand. Eucalyptus trees, native to Australia, are on the rampage around the world. I do not think cooked and chopped garlic has much of a chance in this climate, however. And if it did . . . how wonderful for the hikers to come across fresh cloves of garlic, I fantasise.

"It's heavy," I said.

"I'll carry it," she said firmly.

And we slept, exhausted. Limbs and body aching with the weight of all that water, all that food and all that gear trundled through 16 miles in the hot sun. Sleep says my body; sleep says my mind; sleep . . . .

MEET THE FLINTSTONES

Day 4—42.2 trail miles north
Mount Laguna

I don't sleep well here. Paranoid that animals will steal our food, that people will steal our things, my body lies tense, scrutinising every small rustle. It feels too open, too exposed. What was it that first night—the nimble kangaroo rat, Merriam's chipmunk or a California pocket mouse? Let alone the illegal immigrants, 'coyotes' (the people who pick up the immigrants) and the border control. Kris turned on her torch to go to the toilet in the middle of the night and the hills became alive with signalling. Bird whistles, human whistles, animal noises. Later someone stormed past the pair of us lying on our sheet of building wrap and fought their way into the shrubbery. An American patrol guard getting ready to lie in wait? Or an illegal immigrant waiting for his 'coyote' to give him new clothes, food, water and lead him out into a new life? They caught a group of ten that day. And something that sounded like wild boar snuffled by at dawn. I am scared.

Last night the real coyotes were howling.

We walk. The time passes. The countryside merges into one mass of blur outside the sandy trail where my feet will go. Every step is taken with care and caution. The worst bit is stopping, because then you have to start again and it takes at least twenty minutes to convince yourself that the pain screaming out from each foot is really very low down on the human suffering scale and what are you, a wuss or something? Other hikers pass us and talk of blisters. Kris has them dotted all around the outside of her feet and toes, hard white lumps. Mine have merged into one big squidgy yellow blob beside the joint of my big toe. Are my boots too narrow?

One has to be prepared to change shoes at any instant, says the imaginary voice of Jardine in my head. Leather boots, in the desert, you'll end up crippled, say the 'go-lighters' with authority. There is a PCT story often told (I've heard it several times already from people who've taken one look at my boots and launched into attack mode) of this hiker who wore leather boots all the way and is now permanently crippled. He hobbles around the country giving talks to youngsters, warning them of the danger. My boots cost 100 pounds. They feel special. They are **my** boots; I love them. I can't just forego them, can I?

The path is strewn with lizards and geckoes that scurry out of the way, some leaving grooves in the sand where they have dragged their tails. Somewhere in this landscape are jelamonsters—giant venomous lizards leftover from the dinosaur era, that live hidden in the ground.

We have walked 42.2 miles. That's not a lot.

Kris wants to take a rest day. We're at Mount Laguna, our first mail drop, where we have lost all shame and are trying to go completely Jardine. We sent home extra socks, torches, compasses, spare top and now Kris is even cutting the side off her sneakers (bought because Jardine points out that trainers are lighter than boots, and what you wear on your body, you are effectively carrying) to fit her toes better. This, she claims, is the advantage of cheap gym-shoes; my leather boots are not easily cut. I have to admit to being slightly horrified at the thought. Other hikers who pass rapidly by, keep telling us to cut the spare straps off our backpacks. I would like to lose weight from my pack—they must weigh around five pounds each when empty—but this really seems a bit vandalous.

There's a post office here, a campground and not much else. We are on a budget though, so we don't need much else. Naïvely we think we can just eat our camping food even in town-stops (this will change at the next stop). My blisters are large and unattractive. Everyday Kris and I spend a good half an hour plus sewing holes in our feet, so that the puss can drain out. The idea is to leave the thread in the foot, and walk on it, so that they keep on draining. It's not nice. My back and shoulders are at the point of crunching into a heap of knots and twists that would keep three chiropractors in business for the rest of their lives. Ok, I admit it; I tried to break the end of my toothbrush. Unfortunately my nice, kind, this-is-ridiculous mother made sure that I was well equipped with what she considered essentials, the result is an expensive toothbrush which is designed to bend and won't, therefore, break.

And yet I feel like I'm being reigned in. I feel guilty. You can't stop on Day Four. We'll get behind schedule. We have to keep moving. I can't stop. I must go. Walk walk walk says my mind as though this is some kind of duty one has to fulfil. I'm here to walk. I can't just hang out.

Mentally, I need to be as physically tired as I was on that first day. I want that exhaustion. I want to push push and push until I can go no more. I want to be ready to drop every night. Instead my back hurts in a rather perturbingly unhealthy way, whilst my legs feel barely used. I don't feel stretched. Kris is prickly. I dig myself deeper into unlikely daydreams.

The ladder-backed woodpeckers hammer away at the pinyon pines and squawk noisily, and the jays, a shiny blue with black tufts on their heads, swoop from tree to tree. We spent the day watching the birds and washing socks. And it was good to relax. The post office is a hiker hangout. People queue for the one telephone, exchange blister stories and mileage. They are all lads, boasting of their testosterone, which in this 'sport' translates into number of miles per day. Most of them started at the border the day before. We comfort ourselves with 'it's not a competition' thoughts.

And then there is water. A great lady turned up just to tell us which 'cricks' (as they call them) still had water and where they had cached water for us.

"There's 29 gallons before that gate, 40 gallons up by so and so," she said, pointing at the map sprawled out on her car bonnet. It's amazingly hospitable. People just drive out and hoist gallons of water up into the hills for the hikers.

"We hid it so the illegals won't find it," she chirruped. As you walk you come to signs scratched in the dust or written in sticks: 'H2O →'. We're still carrying about five litres each though, which adds a chunky 11 pounds on to the pack-weight. The scariest bit is yet to come—the views today were out over the scorching Colorado desert and in the next day or two we have to descend from our mountain haven (90 degrees by 9 a.m.) and cross the dry bottom of San Felipe Valley.

Day 7—78.1 trail miles north
Scissors Crossing

So it's a fairly typical day. We have walked about six or seven miles and it is 10.30 in the morning; we stop to have a break and eat some nuts. I find this enormous rock for us to shelter under—the last bit of shade for miles and we crawl in. First things first and the blisters come out to be inspected and aired. Every minute or so the ground is banged with a pole to keep the rattlers away (rattlesnakes are deaf, they react to vibrations in the ground). Not that we've actually seen any yet, but Kris is taking no chances. Kris sits on the rock and I sit beneath the rock on the earth. We eat nuts—soya nuts today, which turn out to be like big dry lentils. That is, we force soya nuts down our poor dry throats into our poor dry stomachs. We rest for about an hour then decide to leave. Something becomes obviously, painfully wrong—my shorts are stuck to my bottom. Not by one small thing, but by millions, trillions of tiny tiny cactus spines. Ow. Well the shorts had to come off, no way round it, and there I was tenderly extracting each and every spine by feel, when round the corner comes a jolly hiker wearing a wide-brimmed floppy hat.

"What you do?" he asks, astonished, in a thick French accent.

"Um, errr, well, we're sheltering from the sun," I say, frozen into position.

Well we were, amongst other things.

"Ahh!" he says, "You are Engleeeesh."

And that explained everything.[2]

They call cactus spines 'stickers' here. And there are oh so many different types of stickers from the 'never-fail', to the 'stick and stay-on' to the 'stick while you wait', 'stick em dead' and even the 'democratic sticker'. All the above seem to apply to my stickers.

One of many types of 'stickers'

It has been a day of incidents. We crossed the San Felipe Valley, panicked for a bit when the water wasn't quite where it was meant to be, and stumbled on to the creek of the same name, which unbelievably was still flowing. Here you have two bedraggled hikers who have not washed for six days (cached water can only be used as desperately needed drinking water). So the clothes came off: socks, bra, top, sarong, and shorts. That's everything. So what to wear while you're washing? A headscarf. Obviously. So there I am scrubbing away daintily and ladylike under a headscarf when three beefy Americans stride round the corner.

"I'm English?" say I (well it worked the last time).

But they studied the ground intently and bumbled on by. Kris now claims that if we are ever in need of help, all I have to do is start undressing, and someone will appear . . . .

We are at present sitting with our feet in the stream. Kris has hurt her ankle or tendon or some such body part. She is sewing her shoes, not, I hasten to add, back together, but replacing the duct tape which she'd put round to stop the stones getting in. She has cut a small corner off our building wrap which she is sewing into her trainers with dental floss. Ray Jardine would be proud of her; hell, *Blue Peter* would give her a job.

Here is Scissors Crossing where several main roads and the trail cross the San Felipe Creek. Kris is wearing slightly more than I am. In fact Kris has a spectacular non-hiking outfit which consists of a jungle sarong tied around the neck which just covers the body, turquoise aqua socks and a blue bandanna. On the grounds of modesty, I send her off to hang our clothes up on the gate by the roadside. She astonishes some of the drivers into swerving as they see what can only be described as Wilma from *The Flintstones* draping bras, shorts and socks over the gate.

We retire to relax under a tree, at last thinking ourselves free from human invasion. The wash has been in vain, the dust is insidious and we are quickly coated with a fresh layer of orange powder as the wind blows our bits and pieces all in their zip-lock bags flying to cling to the nearest cactus. And then there's a surreal moment when a helicopter appears out of nowhere and circles us so closely that we can make eye contact with the pilot. This is a strange country.

That night I am even more paranoid than usual, sleeping right beside a road with helicopters swirling around. I am grateful for our lack of a tent which makes us less conspicuous. (We haven't attempted to put the tarp up again, actually we haven't even dared mention the word 'tarp', and just sleep out under the stars.) Kris can't believe I have never seen a shooting star and calls me a 'city kid' with some contempt. That's fighting talk. It does seem to be rather an embarrassing gap in my ever-so-countrified upbringing— almost as bad as my lack of camping skills. I take my contact lenses out and realise I can't see any stars let alone ones that are dying. This could explain quite a lot.

It's too hard to sleep. The traffic grows less and less and by midnight it is almost quiet. And that's when the headlights swoop over our sleeping-bags and pull off the road to park just twenty feet away. They just miss illuminating our horizontal figures and light the shrub behind us. Two doors slam and the glow of cigarettes act out a complicated, violent dance through the air. There is an argument going on in low muttered voices. I strain to hear if they are speaking English or Spanish but can decipher nothing. I put my glasses on silently and wake Kris. We lie, rigid, unnerved.

Probably they have every excuse to be here—a hundred innocent explanations should be possible, only I can't think of any of them right now. And why would they be interested in two scruffy hikers anyway? Time ticks by and Kris goes back to sleep. Sleep is very important to Kris, even the thought of being hacked to pieces beside a road somewhere not that far from San Diego doesn't stop her sleeping. Or maybe she's just a whole heap more sensible than me. I stay awake and watch. Cigarette after cigarette dances around, sometimes inside the car, sometimes outside, sometimes walking towards us, sometimes away from us. Are they waiting for someone? Coyotes picking up illegals? Drug dealers waiting for cocaine brought all the way from Colombia?

Sleep is a luxury that people in houses can afford. The grime of not washing for six days through the sweltering heat has yet to get to me (it will), although I have to separate my thighs at night which is quite a challenge in a straight-jacket sleeping-bag, to try to find relief from the chafing from my shorts. The dry nuts and unappetising peanut butter has yet to get so completely revolting that I can't stomach it (it will). Even blisters don't seem too bad. But sleep . . . sleep. I crave sleep.

At around 4.30 a.m. they slam the doors, reverse and drive back on to the road. All that for nothing. At five I wake Kris up to her usual grunts—Kris, it has to be said, is not a morning person. I bully and push and sometime after six we leave, laden with water, to climb up out of the valley into the shadeless hills.

We walk our 13 miles to the next water cache. Only there is no water left, just gallon bottles all tied together hanging around the bottom of a giant asparagus that looms taller than everything out of the orange hills. This is actually a Desert Agave, a plant that grows 10 to 15 foot tall. Once in a while (between 9 and 20 years), after a rain storm they burst into flower, but otherwise they are tall, straight, giant asparagus. One begins to understand why there are so many alien sightings in the States. There is an option of walking another ten miles to Barrel Spring. Which is not really an option. Or I can walk down off-trail to the W-W Ranch somewhere below us in the scrub. I park Kris under a tree where she rests her ankle and set off down a track with some vague directions in my head.

There's something comforting about walking along a trail, I realise, now off-trail, even an unmarked trail which is little more than a faint groove in a desert. Walking down what was once possibly a dirt road is slightly alarming. You feel lost instantly. Luckily for me, I took all the right turnings and arrived at the ranch. I wandered through the (turned-off) watering system to the huge pile of junk that eventually evaporated into a house + caravan + old falling-apart trucks. The dogs waited in the shadows until I was almost on top of them and then leapt out barking. I stood still. Guns, cowboys and drive-by shootings flashed through my head in one petrifying second. I walked back down the drive. Then thought about Kris and being thirsty. Turned round, walked back up the drive. The dogs growled. I walked back down the drive. This is ridiculous. So I walked instead in the other direction and came upon the ranch house proper and its owner, Richard. Richard was not the kind of guy to participate in a gangland killing. He was a kindly retiring man who became a real Trail Angel. He let me fill up the two four-litre water bags and the two one-and-a-half-litre bottles and then filled up some empties of his own and attempted to drive me back up to the trail. I did try to warn him that the road wasn't really a road, but he determinedly pushed on in the jeep until some scrub-oak came through the glass window, and that convinced him that walking might be easier. It wasn't a whole heap easier—carrying that amount of water in floppy bags uphill for a mile or so is quite taxing.

Will my feet ever be the same again? I guess not. Blisters have formed on top of blisters beside blisters. I have tried to moisturise life back into my heels. Hoping they don't crack, that would be painful. I'm tired. Feet are tired. Bruised. Ingrained dirt, callused feet, raw thighs, worn shoulders. All in a week.

WORDS OF ENCOURAGEMENT

Day 11—112.9 trail miles north
Dry riverbed

That's ten miles a day. Or 12.5 miles a day with two rest days.

Read my first 'words of encouragement' (from a tiny minute little book of the same name that a friend gave me to carry on my journey—it is made up of short quotes from famous people). In it, Maya Angelou says:

> *Life loves to be taken by the lapel and be told: "I am with you, kid. Let's go."*

Kris has a strained tendon in her ankle. Heel to be precise. The urge/drive to keep moving is a hard one to override. Quote is not really applicable in this instance.

I am sitting in a sunny spot on a riverbed, hoping to catch a woodpecker on camera or a rattlesnake passing to curl up in the sun. Rattlesnakes are cold-blooded and so can only move when the temperature is right. They normally emerge early evening (now) when the ground still holds the heat from the sun but is not so hot that they end up roasted—the trail makes a perfect bathing spot for them. Come on then rattlers! The woodpeckers are at least in no short supply and certainly make enough noise. They are different to the last lot, white-breasted. We have parked ourselves a mile outside the community of Warner Springs. We slept almost in town last night but were told to 'move on' this morning; we had been lying on a sacred Amerindian site.

Warner Springs is a very strange place. There is an Indian Reservation, a private club/ranch, a post office, a fire station and a school. The club owns the golf course, restaurant, rooms for 90 dollars and access to the hot springs. Apart from this there are about five houses. We crawled into the golf club looking pathetic and dirty and ate pancakes. American-style pancakes are like outsized drop-scones which come in huge stacks and taste of very little. Then we discovered the toilets had showers in them for golfers, with towels and soap, and life got an awful lot better. Obviously everything is members only, but if you disappear into a bathroom for 15 minutes and emerge wearing the same clothing—who's to tell? (Except by the smell and the fact that my very short spiky hair stands on end each time it's been washed.) It was close to heaven. This was my first shower of the trip, my first shower after 11 days of carrying 50 plus pounds in temperatures well above the 90s. We must have **reeked**.

In Warner Springs there was a whole collection of hikers—numerous guys who all have short hair and sun-glasses, and travel in threes (one group all with their own tents—is that because of smell?). Also Charlie: he leaves his girlfriend, two horses, a mule and two dogs at the trailhead, then drives the horse/home-mobile to the next stop, then cycles back, puts the bike on the mule, and off they go. Then there was John the Irishman, Mike the American, and Darris the Canadian who all met on the bus from San Diego to the border. John is a white-haired, respectable man travelling light at eight pounds but with an enormous blister; Mike is a wise-cracking veteran who was driven off this section by severe snowstorms a couple of years ago; and Darris is a 19-year old hippie chick with an open personality and an unstoppable mouth. Unbelievably, as these guys rounded the corner of Rodriguez Spur (no roads, no nothing) they were met by Jehovah's Witnesses handing out pamphlets—"No thanks, can't carry any extra weight." Then there are the father and son teams (three so far). Father gets up early, starts walking; son gets up later and catches him up.

Everyone hung out by the table at the gas station, casting longing looks at the hot springs over the road. Rumour has it that occasionally the owner descends on a group of hikers and hands out free passes. Some attempted to saunter through the gates looking smooth and confident like rich golfers. They were stopped immediately. Darris went off on a scouting mission. She wandered round the car park and approached single male golfers, smiling coquettishly. It was a nice try, but it didn't work.

These are the first hikers we have spent time with. Others have just passed by, some so intent on their race they do not even stop to say hello—for some people hiking is a competitive sport. It's nice to have other company. Kris needs to talk more about her ankle and I am not a good sympathiser.

"Don't think about it and it will go away," is my best advice.

Shrewdly, she's not really paying this much attention and is bandaging it, icing it and putting it up on the table.

We speculate on the number of people who started, on the number still going, on the number who will make it. As we were sitting there, the table and surrounding area piled high with boxes and backpacks, a lumbering six-foot-plus heavy guy got off the bus. He checked out his hair in the reflection and approached us.

"Where's the PCT start?" he asked.

The table fell silent to take in this tall figure in his jeans and bomber jacket with a daypack. Someone pointed him in the right direction and we all looked at each other. That was *not* a hiker.

Kirk, a physiotherapist, and I, set off to walk the three miles around Warner Springs, a pleasant stroll through green fields. It was like walking in a picture postcard image of England. As we walked we moved on (with some relief on my part) from blisters, backpacks and Ray Jardine, to the hiking lifestyle. Who are all these people hiking? Why are they here? How can they afford it? What jobs do they do that are so easily dropped? Kirk's job means he is self-employed and can therefore stop and start when he likes. He told me he had been feeling frustrated for some time, bored with work, unchallenged, and moaned each day to his wife. One day, she presumably had had enough and told him, literally:

"Go take a hike!"

He took her at her word and chose the longest hike he could find. His wife helped him with the planning and the funding and was now sending his re-supply boxes to him.

"I miss her," he said, "I just want to call her each day and tell her what I saw, how I feel."

Darris is 19, a gap-year kid. That's young out here, very young. John and Mike are both recently retired. And then there are the groups of 20-something boys who come in threes, a lot of them college boys, trying to cram 2600 miles into three months.

What am I? An actress? A teacher? A tour guide? The other hikers presume my youth:

"Are you in school?" they ask.

(The first one to ask did get a shocked "School?!" but now I realise they mean university, college.) Still. I'm almost ten years older than Darris.

When we got back people were offering to swap their food. It seems everyone is tired of their own supplies already. No-one wanted sunflower seeds. Or peanuts. We scrounged food from the meagre supply at the gas station and ended up with frozen burritos. They tasted fantastic.

I can still taste them now. Tomato/bean mush. Hmmm. The woodpeckers are hammering, squawking from one dead tree-trunk to the next, but no rattlesnakes have emerged. The hikers have all gone on.

"See you down the trail!" they say.

But most likely we will never see them again.[3]

Tomorrow Kris will be ready to try again and I cannot be held down.

Day 12—130.2 trail miles north
Combs Peak

Warner Springs is left behind and we climb up into the hills, out of the chaparral into wild lilacs and pine trees. About five miles up I round a corner to cross a stream and there, sitting on a rock, holding an empty water bottle was the awkward city guy from the gas station who had left two days previously. Five miles in two days? He was sunburnt and looked tired. He leered up at me.

"Are you alone?"

Kris arrived to give the answer and we crossed the stream and walked quickly on.

"Let's keep moving," I said.

I don't think of myself as a particularly paranoid person. I would say 'realistically cautious'. I'm prepared. Many would say paranoid. But then many would also not be here. Fresh in our minds is the story of the two girls murdered on the AT last year, and of the hiker who was mugged on the PCT just north of where we are by two men only a week ago. This hiker was an ex-marine and he barricaded himself into a cabin and stayed awake on guard all night.

The roads are too close, and not close enough. People know who we are from our fundraising web site which is linked to the PCTA web site. Once, we rounded a corner and met four guys coming in the other direction;

"Oh you're the girls hiking for Bolivia, one's from England, one's from Canada," they said.

It's disconcerting.

"You're girls," someone told us. "What do you expect?"

Yes, we're girls. Women, actually, out here alone. Weak, defenceless? I don't think so. Strong, prepared. I'm starting to feel stronger than ever before. We have done steady miles with good breaks and my blisters are healing. My feet are toughening, my leg muscles growing, and even my back is getting slightly more used to its load. I am ready for the mountains. But is Kris?

I think we both feel protective over each other. Both feel responsible for the other one. This could be teamwork, or arrogance: *I am stronger than she is; I must look after her.*

I *am* stronger. I think I am fitter now too. I am also better at handling things like snakes and lack of water. Kris is fearful. She is not happy here, not comfortable, not excited. The new dangers are too real for her, not challenges, but dangers. It takes a certain kind of bloody-mindedness to do something like this. We both have plenty of that. But it takes a whole lot more to do it and enjoy it. She is the more experienced in many ways (with bears, with forests, with water) and reminds me rather a lot. Perhaps her experience is a hindrance not a help. Relax, Enjoy! But the frown is grooved across her face and the grunts monosyllabic. I feel like I'm carrying her, dragging her, forcing her to walk.

We walked until we came to a dirt road. There was, it said in the book, a water tank along this road. I set off, leaving Kris sheltering behind bushes. The large silver tank looked like a shuttle ready for take off in amongst the shrubs. It took me ten minutes to get to the road which had a chain across it, with a dangling notice saying:

Private Property
Trespassers Will Be Prosecuted

Now this is not a notice to be taken lightly in the States. But the footprints I was following clearly continued after the chain. It must be all right. The dogs began barking the closer I got and there, sprayed on to the tank, graffiti-style was:

TAKE WATER AND GO!

DO NOT DISTURB OWNER

I took the yellowy brown water and went.

Camped on the other side of the road was another slightly odd guy. Someone who spent his life walking. We decided to keep on going and had our longest day yet at 18 miles. We camped with Seth and Rick, a father and son team from Oregon, up on the slopes of Combs Peak. Safety in numbers, perhaps I could sleep tonight? There were clouds building in the distance and it seemed necessary to mention the dreaded T-word. We put it up. Or rather Kris put it up and told me what to tie where. Annoyingly it didn't actually rain, but the wind blew all night and kept the tarp flapping noisily. I have not taken to this tarp.

The next day we crawled miserably back down into the hot dusty chaparral. Evidence of wild horses lay scattered around. Kris was silent and unhappy, frowning constantly.

"You're in pain."

"Yes," she said looking worried.

"Let's go to Anza. We'll go to Anza and we'll stay a minimum of five days."

She agreed without a fight. She must have been hurting a lot.

Kamp Anza was not on our original itinerary as it is five to six miles off-trail, but we had heard lots about it from the other hikers. On arrival at the turn-off point by Tule Spring there was the sound of an approaching vehicle. Swirling out of the dust like a stunt man on the *Dukes of Hazard* came a long-haired big-bellied biker on a 'trike'. (This is a three-wheel vehicle that resembles a tractor-style lawn mower only with a very powerful engine. They are now illegal.) He swivelled to a stop and I put on the damsel-in-distress look ("my friend's hurt her ankle, she can't walk, *please* help us"). He installed Kris behind him and they zoomed off back down the track. And then the brain cells began clicking. Had I, the girl who refused to let Kris hitch-hike alone, who stayed awake every night paranoid about crazy people, had I really just persuaded my hiking partner to go off on a three-wheel vehicle with a stranger in the middle of nowhere? I started walking at a ridiculously fast pace in the direction they had gone, eyes glued to the tracks to make sure he hadn't strayed off the road. I consoled myself with the thought that Kris had hiking poles that were really pretty sharp. And then after a mile of pacing, the engine noises returned. My turn. Now this trike, illegal trike, is designed for one person. Not two and a backpack. And Mr. Bikerman was very happy to show off to the girls. Some 20 minutes of clutching on to a beer belly while we twisted round corners at ridiculous speeds, got us storming down the one road of Anza. He pointed out Kris to me just ahead and turned into a driveway. And drove straight into the garage. I leapt off the bike and practically ran outside where I was met by several very well-trained mastiffs. This was not a good situation. Mr. Bikerman was merely changing vehicle however, and we drove the rest of the way in his jeep. Good thing that people are more often angels than not.

Now we are at the 'Hiker's Oasis' in Kamp Anza. Anza and Terwilliger (which sounds to me like an exotic caterpillar) are mobile home communities. They sprawl out in the Anza-Borrego desert in between the odd bit of shrubbery. Hummingbirds hover in front of your face like miniature helicopters, checking you out and then swoop off to a real flower.

Here with us are Doc Rudy, an ex-pilot and sociology teacher, Mudflap, an ex-elephant groom, two Swiss bricklayers, and an investment banker, all hiking the trail, all here due to injury.[4] Here to look after us are Paul and Meadow Ed, two Trail Angels. Paul barks and growls all day:

"Soaking your feet! Get up and hike!"

But he is the first to provide the weary hiker with a bucket full of water and Epsom salts—a real softie at heart. He was born and brought up here in Kamp Anza. Meadow Ed is the Kennedy Meadows Trail Angel, so hopefully we will be seeing him again.

There are three rules on the board. Number two says:

> Duct tape is like The Force, it has a light side, a dark side, and it holds the world together.

Kris has sent us duct tape in each box wrapped around a pen. It definitely holds much of the hiking world together, not least our feet . . . . Everyone has their own cup and we sit drinking juice all day. Conversations, as usual, centre around feet. After that it's start date and finish date, and then backpacks and food. Names come a lot later.

While we are here, we chip in. I ask what I can do.

"You can make tea and put it out on the laarn."

"Lawn?" I question.

Meadow Ed looks at me and points at the small square of neatly fenced green around which our building-wrap has been circling each night in order not to leave a brown patch. Outside the fence everything is dust interspersed with the odd scraggily scrub oak for as far as the eye can see.

"No, I mean, we're going to drink tea on the lawn?"

(In rural California they 'have tea' on the lawn? Like an eighteenth century tea-party? Little finger raised and all? Surely not.)

"To stoo," says Meadow Ed, "put it in the sun to stoo."

"To keep it warm?"

"Waarm?" says Meadow Ed. "Haven't you ever made tea? I thought the tradition came from England?"

He picked up a large plastic jug, flipped up the lid, threw in two tea-bags, opened the freezer and filled it with ice-cubes and then poured in water.

"Now, that goes on the 'lorn'. Should be ready in a couple of hours. Remember to move it so it doesn't get too woorm!"

"Right."

Iced-tea is not just all the rage in California, it's like the state drink. In the shops here, the fridges are lined with various brands and flavours of canned iced-tea—yes, you can get fizzy rhubarb iced-tea to bubble gum flavour to whatever you imagine. Iced-tea is to the south-west coast what 'cworfee' is to the north-east and has been extremely popular ever since the area was 'settled' in the 1850s.

And how did it get here?

Clippers.

Clippers. Nothing to do with barbers or nails. The clipper of 1845 was a fantastic invention—up there with sliced bread—that revolutionised North America. The clipper was a tall dashing young ship that doubled the speed of sailing and it all came about because of Chinese tea. Chinese tea was a much-desired item but being a perishable good was not available. The new speedy clipper (it could do New York to San Francisco at the lightning speed of 89 days and eight hours) meant that the tea could arrive fast enough to be consumed.

Iced-tea on the lawn. This is definitely an oasis.

Day 18—153.7 trail miles north
Pines to Palms Highway

We stayed in Kamp Anza for five days, at the very generous hospitality of Paul. Kris's foot has been mending and things are looking good. On the fifth day we walked the 16 miles around Anza without our packs ('slack-packing' as it is known) but still carrying enough water for the two of us which weighed a good 20 pounds. Half way along was the same city guy from Warner Springs. His face was blistered and he was dehydrated. We gave him food and water and pointed him in the direction of town.

"It's cold at night," he said.

Well it would be, without a sleeping bag. What was he doing here, wandering around the hills? Escaping from something or someone? You can't force someone to leave the trail however inappropriately they are dressed.

Five days. Hikers arrive at Kamp Anza and leave. Nobody says anything but there is doubt written all over their faces, which Kris feels. She is not happy. I try to tell her encouraging things like I know we will make it, that I'm not doing it without her. Although I'm already thinking it would be better if she stopped; stopped and rested for a week, two weeks, got better and came back to meet me further up the trail. Everyone we talk to suggests this. I worry she will think I don't want her around anymore. I tell her even more strongly that I can't go alone, that I'm walking with her and I'm walking to Canada. I am too convinced that everything will be all right because *I know* I am walking to Canada. I still feel incredibly focused and wake up each day ecstatic to be there, raring to get going. Kris is unhappy and depressed. I think that she doesn't want to be here, that it's not what she expected.

We talk. Finally we are talking. She says she does want to be here. It is just her ankle that is bothering her. Perhaps things will be better from now on. I want the laughter, the excitement; I want to share this experience which we've been dreaming about for so long, in enjoyment. It must be a team. We must be equal players in a team. Not one indebted to the other, not one superior to the other. Now is the time to try out any theories of changing one's environment through desire. I *will* be positive. I *will* be inclusive. I *will* bite my tongue. I will listen and be as nice as possible. Actually this won't be equal at all because I will do/be whatever it takes to make Kris feel better about herself. She is in pain, she needs me to be stronger: this is teamwork.

At least, that's what I reason.

We leave again: me blindly hopeful; Kris attempting to be pukka.

Day 20—164.4 trail miles north
Cedar Spring

Our daily routine: six o'clock get up, pack, eat muesli, leave sevenish. Walk until 12.30-1 p.m. with Mars bar break (Kris managed to get 288, or one per hiking day, donated) and nut or seed-of-the-day break mid-morning. Then we eat lunch: spaghetti or soup with rice. Every recipe has sesame seeds and flack seeds (good for the bones), an inhumane amount of garlic topped up with garlic powder. Recipes include gems such as asparagus and coconut soup with pumpkin seeds, or spaghetti and soya nut delight. Kris has planned everything so we have the right amount of calories, the right amount of protein, the right amount of minerals and vitamins and irons; if we eat it all.

Then after a siesta we start up again, about 3.30 p.m., and walk until around seven o'clock with a dried fruit break mid-afternoon. Then we have peanut butter and crackers and two cookies for supper whilst hibernating in our sleeping bags.

All this depends on water. Today around mid-morning there was water at Apache Springs, half a mile steep descent off-trail. Before setting off by myself, I told Kris to watch out for rattlesnakes, not because I thought she'd be in any danger, but I'm desperate for a good photo. So down through the mountain misery—a miserable plant that viciously attacks your legs. I arrived at the trickle and began to pump water up into our water bags through the filter. This is a fairly lengthy process. A hummingbird with a shiny red head and green body came to peer at me.

Another hiker appeared. We went through the usual questions and then the conversation turned to wildlife.

"Seen any rattlers?"

"No, lots of other snakes (five so far) but not rattlesnakes."

"Me neither, scaring us for nothing those guide books."

Said the usual "See you down the road" and started scrambling back through the overgrown misery. Being a miserable kind of plant it had grown right across the path so it was a case of scratching and tearing my way through whilst struggling to hold on to two four-litre bags of water.

"R-r-r-r-r-r-r-r-r!"

Unmistakable. I gave a yelp and leapt back a pace or two and there, where my leg had been, was this thick plastic-white rattle sticking straight up out of the misery. I stared into the bush and made out the tail of a large black and white mottled rattlesnake, about as thick as my wrist. Where was the head? I stamped a lot and eventually it slid away and left me to the miserable mountain misery and a steep rocky climb back up the hill.

Yesterday and today we climbed up along the desert divide into the San Jacinto Wilderness. The trail creeps along mountain sides between huge boulders and burnt pine trees. Last week Marge, a 72-year-old section-hiker (as opposed to thru-hikers like us who hike the whole thing in one go) fell here and broke her leg trying to complete her final section of the PCT. It was two days before anyone found her and she was down to her last cupful of water.

It was a good wildlife day; saw a small herd of mule deer and an owl as well as the usual array of chickadees, jays, woodpeckers and lizards: black ones that do press-ups, green ones with black necklaces, sand-coloured, smaller than a finger ones. The book tells me they are leopard lizard, sagebrush lizard, western fence lizard, desert spiny lizard, coast horned lizard, and, rather magnificently, Gilbert's skink. Now we are camped on Red Tahquitz Peak at 8400 feet, hiding among the red granite from the wind.

Kris appears to be walking well. Her melancholy disposition would suggest otherwise, however. We struggle on often in silence. I stop and wait for her every five, ten minutes, just to make sure she is coming. Just long enough to feel how heavy my pack is. What else can I get rid of? Things can only get better.

Day 21—176.8 trail miles north
Red Tahquiz Mountain

Down, up, round, up, down, round. Guess that's the next six months mapped out. The graph for Southern California in the *Data Book* (small book that has the mileage and height of each place) looks like a plan for the ruins of a turreted castle:

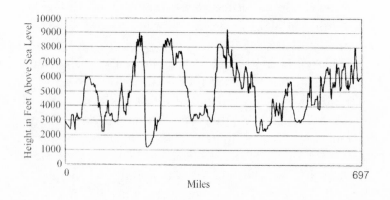

Graph for Southern California[5]

The guide book warns of snowstorms and water shortages in the same section. Today was down from Tahquitz, up from Saddle Junction with good views of Tahquitz (Lily) Rock, down to Strawberry Cienaga (meaning 'swamp' though there wasn't much evidence of one), round to Fuller Ridge. We saw and crossed our first snow and there was a magnificent sunset, possibly due to the Los Angeles/San Diego pollution, but stunning all the same.

Campo, Lake Morena, Burnt Rancheria, Mount Laguna, Rodriguez Spur, San Felipe, San Ysidro, Agua Caliente, San Jacinto—all these Spanish names a reminder that 200 years ago California was settled by Spaniards, initially Franciscan Friars (hence San Francisco). These were a particularly fervent bunch who despite being avid practitioners of self-flagellation managed to convert 40 per cent of the rapidly dwindling native population to Catholicism. After the guilt-ridden, fanatical Franciscans, the next wave of immigrants were a bunch of Mexican rancheros who lived a life of debauched excitement: bull-baiting, dancing, gambling, and hard-drinking, while they worked the Amerindians as slaves on their estates.

Migration from the east began in increasing numbers after Mr. John A. Sutter 'found' The California Trail but even when California declared itself an independent republic in June 1845, hastily sticking a Grizzly and a star on a white sheet (which would later become the state flag), there were still between eight to twelve thousand of Spanish descent, and only eight hundred from the east.

Now, the hispanic presence in rural California is here and not here. The names, the hacienda-style ranches, the food—everywhere you go there are Mexican restaurants. But where are the people? Piles of clothes, rumours of families living in abandoned huts, warning signs in Spanish. 46.7 per cent of the Californian population is now white, and 32.4 per cent hispanic, according to the US Census Bureau. By 2025 it is expected that there will be more people who speak Spanish as a first language than English. Where are they all? Not in the rural communities, that's for sure.

We have just filled up with seven and a half litres each from the San Jacinto River—it's 22 miles to the next water and dehydration is a serious thing. At least one hiker we met had to be air-lifted off the ridge above Scissors Crossing due to lack of water.

"What if we run out of water and dehydrate?"

"What if a rattlesnake bites one of us?"

"What if . . . ?"

Kris is determinedly pessimistic. I would laugh if she wasn't so unhappy. It *is* ridiculously hot and we have to remind each other to drink. Humans drink only to keep their mouths and throats wet and, unlike other mammals, have no inclination to drink because they need to rehydrate. I've heard it said that three quarters of all headaches are caused by dehydration and relief comes more from the glass of water taken with the aspirin than the aspirin itself. Ever cautious of diuretics, we have neither coffee nor tea with us. Instead we have water mixed with powdered juice mix which is supposed to replace the sugars we have lost through sweat, but tastes horrible—an indication, I think, that my body does not need it. So all Kris's carefully weighed out amounts of passion-fruit powder go unappreciated, especially when on leaving a water source late afternoon we forget that breakfast will come in between then and the next water source and automatically fill all our water bags with the juice mix. Granola and passion-fruit sweetened water. Hmm hmmmm.

Kris is going even slower, scared of snakes. I want to run all the way down. The tap and tank shine out from the bottom of the valley and the heat is incredible. I feel fine, just very hot. Kris has not drunk enough. She is worried for me.

Finally we arrive at the haven of a tap at Snow Canyon Road. Yes, believe it or not, there is snow in the canyon, just a wee way back up on the scarred face of San Jacinto, but down here even the breeze is stifling. Three more rattlers this morning. And looming in front of us is the snow-capped peak of San Gorgonio, only first we have to walk across the desert floor of the Coachella valley, where there is the world's largest wind-farm, then up through the chaparral and finally into the shade of the mountains.

We try to construct shade by putting the tarp up (its third appearance on the hike so far), but it's actually hotter underneath. We douse ourselves over and over in water, drinking in relief and drying instantly. It's half past ten in the morning. We rest for an hour, but it's too hot to relax. Very uncomfortable. We can sit here until six this evening and then walk across to a house known as the Pink Motel and rest there. Or we can go now. It's three and a half miles to the Interstate. That's nothing. An hour and a half flat walking. I persuade a reluctant Kris to go.

The first mile is easy, a saunter down a road. Now, feeling fine, with lots of water, we have two and a half miles to go. The next half mile things get harder. We struggle through the sand and it's hot. I am tired. After a mile the path peters out into a warren of jeep trails and motorbike tracks. The book says to follow the posts, but the posts seem to have vanished. I follow the horse tracks. Who else but Charlie and girlfriend, Lady Godiva, could have made these tracks? Who else would be mad enough to ride a horse across this desert? The hoof marks will lead us to the bridge under the interstate. We trudge on, Kris slowly, me stomping furiously. My mind says 'you must arrive'. I am panting, exhausted. Drinking, but my heart is racing. We collapse by a rock that has a foot maximum of shade and drink Gatorade (an energy drink). Kris is quiet and subdued.

"You were right, we shouldn't have gone."

"I know," she says miserably.

I turn my head slightly and for the first time notice a snake just inches from my hand. It looks at me as if to say, 'In this heat? You must be joking.' Neither snake nor I have the energy to move. Eventually we shift again and stop after another half mile by a bush which has vague strands of shade from its thin branches. We have run out of Gatorade. Heat exhaustion hits.

The last half mile is easier and the Interstate welcome. We crawl under the rail bridge to discover a hiker called Mike already collapsed and panting in the sand. Mike is an Englishman who hiked the trail in 1996 and is back to do the odd section (wouldn't this be a bit to miss out?).

We could have died today. My fault. So Kris is right to be so fearful. But I don't think she's going to make it to Canada. I think I'm waiting for the time when she says, "I can't go on, I'll rest" or something. I know I can go alone now. Actually I think it would be easier. Much less to worry about. Little to be responsible for. But then this is *our* trip, *our* adventure, *our* dream. And she has done so much planning and preparation. I want her to get better, be happy and walk with me to Canada. But I don't think she wants to be here. Her pride and sense of responsibility towards me seem to be all that's keeping her here.

We sit and relax for a while and then wander on to find the Pink Motel. Our instructions are a little unclear and we approach several pink houses in confusion, but then Helen and Don Middleton, Trail Angels, come to the rescue with ice-cold water and the right place. The Pink Motel is a pink house held together with all sorts of unlikely things and piled high with sofas. Here is the lowest part of the trail and temperatures are 110 degrees in the shade today. When it's not this hot, it's so windy that you can't walk and the sand stings your body, our hosts tell us. We eat crisp sandwiches and drink from cans in the cool box and laugh for the first time in a while. The shower is a hosepipe that runs hot, boiling hot, from about ten o'clock onwards as it is blasted by the sun. We wash our clothes and leave them out to dry and collapse on sofas. Thank you very much for Trail Angels.

HEAT

Day 23—213.5 trail miles north
Cabazon post office

"Hello, I'd like to send a letter to England please."

"England," thumbing through the book, then glancing at my envelope, "UK . . . ."

"Yes, the UK."

"No," thumbing through the book again. "No honey, that's gotta be Germany."

"Um, no, no, the UK."

"No, it's gotta be Germany. Ukraine? You can have the Ukraine?"

"No, England, the UK, Great Britain."

"Hmm," looking through the book again and then very slowly, as if said for the first time ever, "Great Britain and Northern Ireland."

"Yes, Great Britain and Northern Ireland."

"Okay!" (Tone—if you really want to, but I still think it's Germany.)

Hot hot hot. Hot as a raging furnace. Left late afternoon and dogged up through a skyline of crazy windmills to arrive at a suitable camping place at eight o'clock, nightfall. When the moon comes out, it is ridiculously bright, so bright you can't sleep, but between 8 and 11 p.m. it's dark. Then the next morning, at 5.30 when we left, it was already like a freak heat-wave in London in August and the sun wasn't even up. Ploughed on to reach the Whitewater River by seven o'clock, our first 'river' and not really worthy of the name, though in the wet season it is apparently a gushing torrent. Now the half-mile wide riverbed is covered with knee-high foliage: bladderpod and catclaw, fiddleneck and foxtail. Still, enough water, just, to strip off and sit in—a bath!

Filled up with water for the next 12 miles (a litre every three miles). Kris is terrified of running out of water. She has had the experience of being seriously dehydrated before and does not want a repeat occurrence. I am happy-go-lucky. I just feel that we will be all right, or will worry about it when it happens. Having learnt my lesson from two days ago, I walk leisurely through the heat, letting it dictate my pace. It feels good. Life feels good. There is a hill to climb and ridge to walk along. My muscles feel like they are being tested for the first time on the trip—that's to say, I can feel my muscles stretching over and above the pain from my feet or my back. We clamber on up, me hoping that some of these good feelings will transmit themselves through the airwaves and infiltrate Kris's dark humour. I am falsely cheerful and she knows it. The views are over 180 degrees—a panorama of heat haze from Mount San Gorgonio (11,999 feet) round to Mount San Jacinto round to the desert.

They have predicted record temperatures of 120 degrees (45 degrees centigrade) in Palm Springs today. It is incredibly hot. Nothing moves, no lizards dart through the sand, no bladderpods blow to the floor; there is a hot silence. I stop to wait for Kris often and we take breaks, reminding each other to drink, nibbling on salted sunflower seeds to keep up our energy levels. She's hot and she doesn't function well in the heat. We are running low on water. In fact we are down to our last half litre and we've only done six miles. It's also getting late in the day—11.30 a.m. By noon it will be just too hot. Finally we get off the ridge and start descending into the valley of Mission Creek. Below there are trees, willows and baccharis crowding the valley floor. This is a good sign, where there are trees there is usually water. Let's hope it's surfacing water. Again I get the urge to run all the way down the many zigzags but know I must wait.

We get to the bottom and follow the trail for what seems like an endless winding and twisting with many false hopes and disappointments when we reach yet another dry stony creek bed. Luckily the last one prevails: water.

"Water!" I shout joyfully.

This could be the tonic Kris needs. The water is a trickle but in our hot sweat we lie down in it, letting the coldness flow along our backs, sending the pond-skaters flying. We siesta-ed for over five hours until the heat was just that bit less intense, and then continued the journey on up beside Mission Creek.

Day 26—234.3 trail miles north
Mission Creek

Today is a bad day. Woke up to find my eye puffed up like a balloon, possibly due to the sweat and sunscreen pouring down my face the day before or maybe something bit me in the night. Looked around to find everything crawling in ants. They had got into my toilet bag (what you bring in, you take out, including used toilet paper—*nice!*) and were swarming everywhere. Felt grumpy and grim and we set off late—after seven o'clock. Feel like I am the sole source of energy here. If I don't get up then we never would, if I didn't go then we would never get anywhere. Want, just for this one day, for someone else to be the input, carry the weight; I too need encouragement. I don't say any of this to Kris, using the walking to pound it out of the system. Way too hot. Walked for five hours but only went five miles according to the book. Can't possibly be right. Plagued by flies that land straight on your eyes and hover in front of your face.

Came across a huge bag of horse-feed that had been ripped open, horse nuts everywhere—a bear? But why leave the nuts? A cougar maybe. Very strange. And why was it there anyway?

Filtering the water and the filter just stopped working. Got to say these Platypus bags are not wonderful. The idea is great—a four-litre bag of water with hose for easy drinking access. The hose drips continuously, which is pleasant when hot, but wastes vital water. Now (as the filter has broken) we've had to put iodine in and therefore powdered juice mix to hide the taste, which means sticky sugar water drips down your shoulder. Also three out of the four bags have got holes in and now the actual pump has broken, too.

Definitely quote time:

> *No life is so hard that you can't make it easier by the way you take it.* (Ellen Glasgow)

Ok, ok.

And be reasonable. You're not the one who's injured.

Finally worked the miles out (the book was wrong) and we had walked eight and a half miles rather than just five. Carried on to arrive at Coon Creek Jumpoff (a hang-gliding place) in the dark. Half-heartedly thought about hanging our food from a tree as we are now possibly in bear country, but we were too tired and dejected. A hard day. Long discussions around the realisation that we are now late and might not make it to Canada. Can we still do it? Even if winter comes late this year, we will not have beaten it. But right now there is the more immediate race of getting to the mountains and out of the heat. It's hot, just too hot, even up at the tree-line. By midsummer the *average* temperature will be 115 degrees (43 degrees centigrade), and in the Mojave it has even hit 132 degrees (51 degrees centigrade).

Kris has been thinking that she won't be able to make it for a while. Been too scared to tell me. I mustn't get down. One despondent person is plenty in a team of two. I must be positive. I must keep going. We will never get to Canada if we don't think it's possible. Can one person believe enough for two? I feel like I'm carrying two people all this way.

Every day it's a new thing in the morning; she's put her back out, she thinks she's getting flu, her ears hurt, she might get sunburnt, she might get dehydrated, she might get this, that, the next thing. I wake up every morning feeling a surge of happiness that makes me smile, then I wake Kris and her misery knocks me down. When we walk I try to be cheery.

"Oh, look at the butterfly!" I cry. "Isn't it beautiful?"

"It's a moth," says Kris.

"The trunks of these pine tress are incredible!" I exclaim. "I took loads of photos."

"They're cedar trees," says Kris.

I come across footprints in the dust, similar to a human but slightly different. It must be a bear, I think, heart starting to pound, a bear! My first bear, are we close? The footprints look fresh, will we see it? Kris approaches.

"Look Kris, a footprint! A bear!" I say.

"It's not a bear," says Kris.

There aren't, however, exactly a lot of possibilities.

"Perhaps it's an escaped dwarf from a circus who lost his shoes," I say.

I am insensitive. Hard. I judge hard and she knows even though I don't say anything.

"Why are you so unhappy?"

We talk long and in earnest. She says that I think she's a hypochondriac. I agree; I do. She says I think her injury isn't real.

And it's not that simple. I do think her injury is real, but I think she pays it too much attention, and that this hike was always going to involve pain. Serious pain. She has strained her tendon, if she wants to walk 2000 miles she must somehow overcome this. If it's really that bad she should rest. Take time out and meet me somewhere later on.

But she cannot compromise. She will walk every step of the way. She just wants to go slower, do less miles.

But that means we have to carry more. And it's getting hotter and we still have to cross the Mojave.

And they said that you had to have reached the Sierras not later than June—maybe the first week of June if you were really lucky—because it just gets too hot. And it's already too hot and she is the one that feels the heat and worries about the water. And the water is now getting further and further apart, and we need to hike from source to source in one day or else double up our water load. And I'm carrying too much.

It's all too hard and I don't want to think about it.

Get better Kris, get happy and walk with me to Canada.

We're passing through gold country—names like Gold Mountain, Prospect Spring, Borrow Pit, and Deadman Canyon appear on the map. Here is Baldwin Lake, named after 'Lucky' Baldwin, who bought the mine for six million dollars and failed to locate any gold, so just why he was so lucky I'm not sure. The original site was around the town of Bellesville, a true wild west town where records show enough people hung and gunned down in the street to make a whole sequence of Hollywood movies. The gold is all gone, the town deserted, the only thing left for the hikers is the pyrite or fool's gold which sparkles in the sand. And all that happened only 150 odd years ago.

Just four hundred years ago, there were around seven hundred thousand Amerindians living in California alone. Six major languages, and one hundred and fifty different societies. Round here there were farming people living along the Colorado River on beans, corn and pumpkins; and people who lived where I'm walking now, in this sagebrush desert, on lizards, insects, snakes and nuts. Has a PCT hiker ever resorted to rattlesnake stew? How would one find meat on the spiky horned lizard?

Horned lizard

The first 'contact' was most likely disease, the second a Spaniard named Hernando de Alarcon who sailed up the Colorado River in

1540, and the third the Spanish invasion, over two centuries later. By the 1840s historians reckon there were only two hundred thousand Amerindians left in California, and this was before settlement, before gold, and before genocide.

Within the next twenty years, California was admitted to the Union, there were some five thousand wagons on the California Trail (which we will cross up near Lake Tahoe) and the non-native population had soared from around 100 to 380,000. And they bulldozed their way through communities and people.

> *The California valley cannot grace her annals with a single Indian war bordering on respectability. It can boast, however, a hundred or two of as brutal butchering, on the part of our honest miners and brave pioneers . . .*

said the nineteenth-century historian H.H. Bancroft.[6] Parties of men would go out two or three times a week to kill 50 or 60 Amerindians on each trip. And all because of gold.

The brother of the Mayor, Don Francisco Lopez, found gold when he pulled a bunch of wild onions from the ground. The yield from the first year, 1842, was estimated to be 10,000 dollars which was a hell of a lot back then. Others were not so lucky. One Fernando was out looking for stray cows on a hot lazy afternoon back around the time when California was still in Mexico. Fernando lay down under an oak tree and dozed off for a siesta. Whilst he slept, he dreamt vividly of gold. Gold chains, gold nuggets, gold rings, gold necklaces, gold cuff-links, gold shoes, and most particularly, of a gold waistcoat. How wonderful it would be if he could swagger into town wearing a gold waistcoat. How handsome he would look! How rich he would be!

The sun moved steadily across the sky until he was no longer lying in the shade of the oak tree. Fernando woke up and rubbed his eyes. It was very uncomfortable where he was lying—a root or something was digging into his back. He sat up and looked around and Cor Blimey! (or probably more along the lines of '¡Ay Caramba!'), if there wasn't just a bar of gold lying right there where his back had been! He picked it up and set off at a healthy lick to the ranch.

"GOLD!!" he announced. "We are RICH!"

You can just imagine it now—they've won the lottery, they got all the numbers and the family sit late into the night. Ma cooks an extra chicken, Pa gets out the best aguadiente, and the slaves even get an extra half-spoon of corn meal.

"I'll buy a new horse, damn it I'll buy a team of horses!" shouts Fernando.

"I'll buy more land, I'll buy the whole valley!" shouts Pa.

"I'll buy more bulls!" shouts brother.

"I'll . . . I'll . . ." shouts Ma.

"I'll buy you a new dress," says Pa patting her on the arm, "and maybe we'll even get the water fixed so it comes into the house."

Wahooo!

So the next day bright and early they all set off at a gallop. They ride for an hour or two. Maybe three.

"Are we nearly there yet?" the small spoilt kid brother whines.

"Just round the corner," says Fernando, his teeth grinding a piece of straw. "Just round the corner."

"There!" he says and swings off the path towards an oak tree.

It's only the third or fourth time, bless, and anyway there's gold at the right one.

"It was somewhere here, I'm sure of it."

The next day they take the foremen and all the slaves and scour every oak tree in sight. By the third day Pa has a plan.

"We'll dig," he says "We'll just dig anyway because gold's under the ground, see."

"Of course!" says Fernando extremely relieved, of course.

So they dig, or rather the slaves dig while they watch. They dig manholes in front of each oak tree, six-ten foot deep. They dig for three to four weeks. Nothing. [*Small note for future hikers: Don't stroll in front of oak trees in the Angeles National Forest, you might disappear suddenly.*] Lost the god-damn lottery ticket and they're not going to give you the money even though they know it's you. Today at least you could sell your story to one of the tabloids, somehow I doubt that the San Fernando Comet (started 1883), had it been in circulation then, would have paid quite so well. No gold.

Modern investigations have since established that there was no gold in that area and it is presumed that Fernando's gold bar which caused him to waste time on dream-coats was actually washed downstream by way of the seasonal Santa Clara River. What you are more likely to come across in the Angeles Forest are corpses. It has, apparently, been a favourite dumping ground for all LA disputes since the 1800s and the forestry commission, I'm told, regularly happen upon a decomposing body.

Here we met Janet, the first hiker we have overtaken (whehey!), dressed head to foot in the GoLite shell jacket and trousers. Janet, not decomposed but not all that composed either, is going so 'light' that she is running out of food. Not entirely unselfishly, we persuaded her to eat some sunflower seeds mixed with chocolate chips. Janet says when she gets to Big Bear City she's going straight to the bigger town of Big Bear Lake to see a film.

"Don't you just miss movies?" she asks.

Janet won't visit Trail Angels and she won't hitch. At her last town-stop she called the local school and got the director/headmaster to take her to town. Teachers apparently can be trusted.

So, pounding down the rocky trail (makes for difficult walking) trying to THINK POSITIVE; I went round the corner and—ohmygod!—it's a bear. A big bear. Ok, bit of a cheat, it's behind a fence; it's a Hollywood bear. Yup, the animal movie stars live out here off a dirt road in the middle of nowhere in quarters infinitely smaller than those of their human counterparts. We did hear that one hiker got so scared—he saw a big bear pacing up and down what looked like a rubbish dump—that he ran off the trail down the road and hitched into Big Bear City.

Finally Thinking Positive. We are going to make it. We have showered, courtesy of the fire-station, and we have eaten a large veggie-burger (no nuts or seeds) and an enormous tub of cookie-dough and chocolate chip Haagen-Dazs ice cream; now about to start on a fresh fruit salad, once our clothes have finished drying. Town-stops are very necessary revitalisers. Tomorrow I get to meet my nephew for the first time and see my brother Ben and his wife Anna Marie who live nearby in Los Angeles.

Thinking Positive!

Charles, a friend of Ben's, came to meet us for the day in Big Bear. He drove us back to the trailhead from where a botanist had given us a lift the day before; left us and drove on jeep roads to a point 16 miles further down the trail; ran, uphill, to meet us as we walked from the other direction; then walked back with us, ran to get the car, chauffeured us to food, and then finally to Los Angeles. Every hiker needs a Charles. In fact, everybody needs a Charles.

It was like we had been beamed to a parallel universe or taken from a future age back into a past one. Everything was familiar but so strange. People in their masses strolled at a queasy pace up and down Venice Beach. Girls with streaming blonde hair and mannequin arms and legs streaked through the crowds on roller-blades. There was selling and calling and buying and laughing and haggling and gestures. Huge cars drifted along streets the width of runways. There was food everywhere and smells and helicopters watching from above.

Kris got tendon treatment from a Chinese masseur. I gawked and gooed at what has to be the most adorable baby ever (I guess all aunts are a little biased). Anna Marie cooked fresh fish with real live vegetables. And then I had a bath. Carpets are sensational.

Then the next day it was Ben's turn to be a star. He took us back to Crab Flats Road, this time with the luxury of a four-wheel drive. I have no idea how Charles' car survived, or Charles for that matter. About two miles into the day, surrounded by burnt willow trees and purple chia, Ben's boots dramatically crumbled and fell apart. Very strange, the soles had just rotted away. Kris did her stuff with the duct tape (the Force) but it was not to be and Ben had to continue with the appearance of a boot strapped around his feet but with no bottom. Lunch was cream cheese and bagels with fresh fruit—we should visit people more often on this trip—and then we carried on alone.

It was a beautiful day; followed Deep Creek down and down through gullies and canyons always with the sparkling water below us. Eventually we came down upon a grassy area close by the water and discovered a large naked Meadow Ed plonked in the water, with another hiker called Jason. Deep Creek Hot Springs. Heaven. Meadow Ed had come prepared with corn-on-the-cob and baked potatoes and chicken. A real Angel. This is getting too good to be true.

We set off with Jason to walk good long days around the rim of the Mojave. Coming down to the Mojave Dam, I was looking back up at Kris, gesturing which path to take, and almost stepped on a large yellow and brown gopher snake. It had just caught a bird and was attempting to digest it, the bird being about three times as wide as the snake's head. It's great seeing wildlife at work. We stood and watched two lizards make love (or war) a couple of weeks ago. They were engaged in some kind of Round Dance/Chase for ages before they finally fastened on to each other's necks in a slow wrestle.

Jason was leading the way. He was about two hundred yards below me on the trail and I could hear the **rrrrrrrrrrrrrrrrrr**. The whole hillside seemed to be rattling. What we had to pass was one very large, very angry, mean-looking rattlesnake who was furious at being disturbed and was not going to budge an inch. I took a hesitant step forward and the head rose up: it was coiled and ready to strike. We banged and stamped and poked and prodded but to no avail. This one was staying put.

Rattlesnakes are all poisonous but not necessarily deadly. They will bite if you step on them or they feel threatened. The problem is the Mojave Green Rattlesnake, whose bite is fatal unless treated within six to twelve hours, but no symptoms show until it is too late. Mojave Greens, however, do not look dissimilar to other types of rattlesnakes (here in California they are all diamond-backed, but come in a wide variety of colours depending on their environment) so if you are bitten, it's fairly disruptive to the hike. The worst ones are the babies because they cannot control their venom and if they bite, they inject the whole load into you.

'*If bitten,*' says the guide book, '*get to hospital immediately.*' The chances of being bitten though are pretty small, even when you're passing six or seven rattlers a day, as the majority are not aggressive.

"Tell that to this one," says Jason.

We eventually passed it by scrambling down the mountain, giving it a wide berth.

We left our packs at the proposed camp, above a high-pressure gas pipe and below an enormous pylon, and nipped down to Interstate 15 and the truck stop; McDonald's—a real wilderness experience this one . . . . I would like to mention at this point that McDonald's is not a normal port of call, but you've no idea just how tempting a milkshake can be after hiking in Southern California.

"Thought you'd be here hours ago!" said a voice.

Meadow Ed is like a garden gnome that someone transplants secretly each night to a new surprising location. He just keeps popping up. He spends each summer following the hikers— bringing them surprises, treats, company, and walking the odd section or two. He has a large scrapbook for hikers to write their comments. And in the winter he goes from friend to friend. The trail is home for him it would seem, and not just for one summer.

Seems strange to be confronting a rattlesnake in the middle of nowhere and then a few hours later washing the poison oak off your legs (a feat!) in the McDonald's 'restroom'. Kris went with Meadow Ed to Wrightwood to rest her feet and pick up our box. This is good, this is sensible. She seems ok, actually she seems a bit better. Since we talked things have improved. In Wrightwood she may be able to find new shoes, some boots which could give her ankle more support. That would be much better. If injuries can be healed by willpower alone, then she stands every chance, as both of us must spend every spare second willing her ankle to grow stronger.

Jason and I crossed under the Interstate where amidst the graffiti, one artist had written:

$$CANADA \rightarrow$$
$$\leftarrow MEXICO$$

Going the right way then.

We tackled the start of the San Gabriel Mountains, 5000 feet up and we could still hear the hum of the cars, while the LA smog crawled along the valleys and round the hills. Then the next day was a beautiful morning with the mist lolling below the Sheep Mountain Range, perfect viewing from our ridge-top camp. Then up into the ski-lift area with a few patches of snow remaining. Blue jays, juncoes, phoebes and that's just the birds. Lupin and paintbrush and purple chia line the path below the pine trees. Pleasant change from the evil poison oak yesterday.

Poison oak leaves its oil on any part of you that it touches and then you transfer it everywhere else. For some people it gets so bad that it means the end of the hike. Kris heard of one woman last year who had the misfortune of peeing in the dark in a poison oak area . . . .

Met up with Kris and Meadow Ed and a hiker called Christopher from the New Forest (Hampshire, England) with a great talent for story-telling, in Grassy Hollows Campground, and with them came apples, bananas, chicken and corn-on-the-cob.

Meadow Ed helped Kris to look for plants to take the place of her Ibuprofen. She has been advised by her father to eat turmeric. Twelve teaspoons of turmeric a day, to be precise. Which is a lot of turmeric.

The next day, a Saturday, we climbed up Mount Baden-Powell (9400 feet) with great views back over Mount Baldy. Endless groups of beefy men dressed in huge boots, short white socks pulled up to mid-calf, beige shorts, T-shirts, caps and day packs, accosted us with endless questions.

"What do you eat?"

"What do you drink?"

"Where do you sleep?"

"How do you get food?"

People from LaLaLand out for their 'back country' experience. The best conversation went along the lines of:

Day-hiker:	"How do you carry enough water?"
Thru-hiker:	"Yes, well it is difficult, back in the desert we had up to eight litres at a time and it was so hot."
Day-hiker:	"Eight litres—how many days does that last?"
Thru-hiker:	"Well it depends on the heat, sometimes just one day."

Day-hiker:	"So you get to a shop every day?"
Thru-hiker:	"A shop? What for?"
Day-hiker:	"Water, I'm asking about water. Where did you get that water you're drinking now?"
Thru-hiker:	"There's a spring just a mile back."
Day-hiker:	"It's not bottled??!?"
Thru-hiker:	"Err, well, no."
Day-hiker:	"Ohmygod, guys you hear this? She's not drinking bottled water . . . you can die you know . . . you ought to be careful."

I did learn, however, from one of the day-hikers that I am now entitled to my Baden-Powell Scout Badge as a result of climbing the mountain. The story goes that back in 1909 an American publisher named Boyce got lost on a 'foggy day in London town . . . '. Probably it was pretty grim—cold, wet and almost certainly the air would have been heavy with the black soot smoke from the coal burning in so many houses and factories (hence the word smog, from smoke and fog). The lost American was truly lost, perhaps panicking slightly as he wandered around the back streets able to see nothing and hear only the muffled sounds of people coughing or coaches passing. As he turned a corner a young boy going in the other direction ran slap bang into him. Mr. William D. Boyce asked for assistance and the boy led him to his destination. Immensely grateful, Mr. Boyce took out his coppers to tip the boy. The boy refused. Who knows if he was proud or offended—there's a whole tipping culture here in the States that I haven't even begun to get the hang of yet—but the reason he gave was "a Scout does not accept gratuities for doing his good turn." The astonished Mr. William D. Boyce quickly asked to know more and, on return to the United States, set up the Scout Movement there.

In a way the 'good turn' mentality has rubbed off into the hiking world. Or perhaps it is the hiking world that gave rise to the good turn—Lord Baden-Powell was after all an expert back-country person. Here the name of the trail is like a password. Say it among other hikers/would-be hikers/hiker support crew and they'll pick you up, drive you around, feed you, give you a bed to sleep in, a bath to wash in. Not one good turn in a day, but all these things for a complete stranger. It keeps astounding me no matter how many times it happens.

It wasn't until 1931 that the mountain was dedicated to 'BP' as Baden-Powell was known. Frederick Burnham, an American who had learnt his scouting techniques from the Amerindians, and who fought with BP in Africa, gave the address.

> *The Scout Movement means much more than sleeping on the cold ground under the stars, or rubbing two sticks together to make a fire . . . In this still troubled world it means keeping alive in the hearts of men the fire that should never die.*[7]

Sexist, racist and a great believer in the wonders of the British Empire, Baden-Powell nonetheless instilled a love of camping and countryside in thousands of people across the world—at the foot of his mountain there were Scouts everywhere. Christopher set about incorrigibly encouraging the stereo-type Americans have of the mad eccentric English Gentleman out in the mid-day sun. Dressed from head to foot in white, and twirling a large Mylar-covered umbrella, he cut a fine dashing figure. He strode through the Scout camp, towering above the little boys who came to tug at his clothes to check if he was real and ask question upon question, digesting the answers in awe.

WATER

Day 41—454.9 trail miles north
Agua Dulce

'*A hot, waterless, dangerous, ugly and entirely un-Crest-like segment of trail*' says the guide book. Oh good! '*Water is the key to all life . . .*' yes, thank you, '*without water you can survive only two days at 120 degrees if you stay in one spot, five days at 100 degrees and nine days at 80 degrees. If you walk during the day you will survive only one third as long.*' These are government figures for someone without a pack. Actual hiking conditions require at least two gallons a day when hiking in 100 degrees heat with a backpack and most people will function better with two and a half gallons. That's ten litres. Ok now for the water availability:

Agua Dulce	*WATER ALERT 22.9 miles*
Lake Hughes	*WATER ALERT 29.6 miles*
Highway 138	*WATER ALERT 16.4 miles*
Cottonwood Creek	*WATER ALERT 22.5 miles*
Cross Oak Spring	*WATER ALERT 24.9 miles*
Golden Oaks Spring	*WATER ALERT 18.3 miles*
McIvers Spring	*WATER ALERT 35.5 miles*

Did I scare anyone yet? And then, if you can carry enough water, there are gusts of wind up to 100 miles an hour including '*swirling dust devils that can send unwary hikers sprawling or ducking for cover behind a grotesque Joshua tree.*' Get the feeling that the authors really enjoyed this section . . . . And then they warn of rattlesnakes, ticks, off-road vehicles and earthquakes!

Luckily for us there are Trail Angels dotted around this area, who leave water caches, shortening the distances to only (*only?*) 20 miles between supplies. At the moment we're staying in luxury at Donna and Jeff's. Donna, who took Kris and me to the border at the start of our hike, has risen from being a Trail Angel to 'Saint Donna, Our Lady of the Laundry'. She takes hiker clothes ingrained with sweat and dirt and somehow manages to reproduce them in their original colour. And she has a stack of blue shorts and white T-shirts for the hikers to wear while their clothes are being washed. There's not exactly a lot left to my legless trousers or my pink vest top, however, to wash—they are more hole than clothing. The back of my top is one big gaping hole, and the straps are no longer straps, just vague bits of string that are completely useless—all worn away by the pack. I hand them over to one of the four dogs waiting to grab a smelly hiker sock. Donna lets me keep a pair of the blue shorts and I have a new blue vest top from the re-supply box. Result: I am now navy blue from head to toe, but who cares? There's the beauty of it.

192 thru-hikers have passed this way so far this year. I am number 193. (One of this year's last thru-hiker's got his trail name at Donna's, becoming '220'.) Donna and Jeff have an elongated mobile home where there are beds with duvets (sleeping in a bed was surprisingly hard), a record-player with some cheesy numbers, a TV and the not-exactly-riveting though aptly named video *Somewhere along the Way*—a tale of two brothers walking the PCT. Separated from our media-based culture for too long, we gorged on movies, takeaway pizzas and beer, pausing every now and then to worry over water and weight.

Christopher has lost 27 pounds since the beginning of his trek. That's a lot, especially as he is bean-pole shaped and doesn't look like he was particularly large to start with. Others too have lost a lot of weight. Rather bizarrely, I have gained weight which, I reckon, is quite an achievement given the conditions, though we are eating a phenomenal amount. The four of us (Christopher, Turtle/Jason, Kris and I) shared a gallon of chocolate ice cream yesterday. Christopher managed to gain back two pounds just from the one day. We said a sad goodbye—will we ever see them again?—

and stayed around to rest for another day. It was just too nice, too comfortable. We were joined by two girls and a boy from South Carolina who wore the rims only of identical straw hats. They seemed to be going at an incredible pace, equipped with state-of-the-art backpacks or rather daypacks that weighed less than a feather, and were planning to take a ten-day holiday from the trail when they got to Walker Pass.

Day 44—516 trail miles north
Highway 138

Full speed into the section: 20 miles, 19 miles, 19.4 miles, measured our first few days. Not bad going, not bad at all. Perhaps we can still make it. Kris is really trying, though the days are very long and we are both exhausted at the end of each one. Walking fewer miles here is not really an option as we have to reach the next water supply each night. And it's not so ugly either, in fact beautiful deciduous woods of sycamore and black oak and mountain mahogany. Came across a nest of ground squirrels (like normal squirrels but with unfluffed tails) and then a field of butterflies.

The guide book tells me that the Pacific Crest Trail was first conceived of in 1926 and by 1937 the trail through Washington and Oregon was established. The trail through California wasn't completed until 1993, however. Some of this delay was due to factors such as World War Two, but most of the delay was caused by arguments over private property rights. Here, the Tejon Ranch finally caved in to years of court wrangling and allowed the trail to skirt around its edges. The writers of the guide book are so angry about this that the pages are nearly growling, and on entry, there is a lovely large sign which gives us a list of all the things we are not allowed to do. Essentially it boils down to 'get through this bit as fast as you can and don't take one step off-trail'. By contrast, the next two days will be full of the famous hospitality and generosity of the American people.

We stopped overnight c/o Jack Fair, a seventy-nine-year-old military veteran. The yellow house is covered in home-made signs. One reads:

Did you forget? We are all so paranoid. There are no free-thinkers left.
The only right of choice is which leg you use to put your pants on first.

The welcoming sign says:

PCT Hackers 509 plus so for.

(The spelling mistakes are unintentional.)

A friend of a friend of a friend of Kris's, Adrianna, came to meet us with her father. Dad and Jack got straight down to serious talk: turns out Jack knew Sonny Barger, big-time Hell's Angel on whom the movie *Easy Rider* was based. Turns out Dad made B-movies for Walt (e.g. the well-remembered *Cotton-pickin' Chicken-pickers*), and shot all the underwater footage for *20,000 Leagues Under the Sea*. Turns out they both knew cats;

"I had fifteen years with big cats," says Jack.

Cats seem to be a big thing round here. Cougars or mountain lions need a vast range in order to survive. A female with cubs kills a deer every three days on average, whilst the male cougar's territory extends from 40 sq. km to 800 sq. km. There are still, however, some five thousand surviving in California despite the encroachment of suburbia. It's hard to comprehend, coming from Britain, just how much space there is here—I've been told you can drive through Montana for a whole day and night, and see nothing: not mountains, not trees, not people, nothing. What does threaten cougars is roads. The Interstates slice through the wilderness and cats die on the road each year. It would be fantastic to see a mountain lion, but very unlikely. Christopher camped down in the valley of Soledad Canyon and heard them roaring at night. Wild mountain lions? No, Tippy Hedron, the star of Alfred Hitchcock's *The Birds*, runs an animal refuge nearby (no birds allowed).

We got the royal treatment from Adrianna and her family. Taken into Lancaster, taken to lunch, queued for our five boxes in the post office, taken home, clothes washed, boxes unpacked and repacked in the beautiful garden, taken shopping, taken back to the post office, taken to the trail. And she's coming again to Tehachapi! We love Adrianna.

Town-stops are not rest days, contrary to what one might expect. Normally they involve unpacking boxes at the post office, taking off your boots to wax them (at the post office), filling up small bottles with lotions and potions and pills from larger bottles in the drift box, and making agonising decisions on whether or not you will need some item of clothing for the next week. Then we have to go through the food for the week; dump in the Hiker Box (a box for hikers' odds and ends) what we can't eat any more of (nuts, seeds), buy what we can eat more of (crackers—Kris, muesli—me). Then go through the section in the guide book to check water supplies and possible hazards: all inside, or sitting on the steps of, the post office.

Lancaster was a cleansing experience. I sent home my poles and my sleeping mat and my re-acquired head-torch and more socks. Bought a new lighter sleeping mat. The Thermarest is infinitely superior—comfortable and warm, but this thin blue bit of sponge weighs next to nothing. We are still carrying too much. My back hurts and the weight puts more stress on Kris's foot. (I learnt rather belatedly that you are not supposed to carry more than a third of your body weight, which for me is 35 pounds. With water and food my pack must have been up to 50 pounds at least and even up to 70 pounds on some days through much of Southern California. No wonder my back hurt so much.) It may cost money, but sending something away feels wonderful, x number of pounds that you won't have to carry.

Set off late in the afternoon to start our plod along the aqueduct. We were thinking of night-hiking and the moon was perfect for it. Ray Jardine warns against this claiming that every stick looks like a rattlesnake. Rattlers do normally rattle to warn you that you are about to get too close for comfort, but then there is the rather alarming factor of the 'silent rattler'. Encouraged by an attempt to pest-control in the 60s, this type perfected the skill of rattling without the noise and flourished as a result of man

killing off all the loud rattlers. Nice try. This is our first real piece
of flat walking. We walked first along one aqueduct, an open one
serving the Antelope Valley which apparently goes so fast that
unwary swimmers often end up 100 miles downstream a little
quicker than intended. We have been warned not to attempt to
get water from it (might lose your bottle apart from anything else).
Nice water these people drink, with 'floaters' (drowned people)
regularly going down. Then on to the closed aqueduct for 20-odd
miles.

Los Angeles has drained its surroundings of water. The
thundering Colorado River that carved out the Grand Canyon is
steadily diminishing. And ahead we will pass by the dry lakebed
of Owen's Lake, once a vast mass of shimmering blue sweeping
across the glaciated valley from the Sierras towards Death Valley,
now a green and red haze of mouldy lichen alongside Highway
395. The 233-mile aqueduct was constructed in 1913 and has
caused endless court battles (which still continue today) and a fair
few shooting sessions, including dynamite attacks, a raid by a 70-
strong band of armed men, and a shoot-to-kill policy by the
government. In 1928 a dam collapsed killing 450 people in the
flood. The green pastures of Owen's Valley are now one big dusty
plain, but still the hungry city is not satisfied. For California
everything depends on the snowfall in the Sierras and weather
stations rapidly measure and calculate just how much Los Angeles
can suck away each year. Apparently they have now got so desperate
that they send tankers up to the Arctic to steal icebergs. Those
Hollywood stars have got to keep their swimming pools full.

We walked into the night appreciating the coolness and decided
eventually to park ourselves somewhere off the aqueduct in the
scrub, only to find the sand saturated with the fine needles of
cactus spines.

"Let's just sleep on the aqueduct," said Kris.

This didn't sound ideal to my paranoid mind. Visions of groups
of disaffected youths from the mind-boggling A-Z, 1-90 street
system of Lancaster/Palmdale cruising out along the aqueduct to
drink beer and shoot at random targets, floated before my eyes.

The centre of the one-storey high town is Wal-Mart. Where do you go when you've nothing to do? Wal-Mart. Adrianna's parents had a permanent note on the door which read 'If we're not in, we're at Wal-Mart'. Apparently they now have hook-ups so that people can tour round the country in their mobile homes and become 'hooked-up' to Wal-Mart wherever they go. That would be enough to drive anyone out into the desert to shoot at litter and PCT signs and/or the odd hiker or two. But there was nowhere else.

We had the usual discussion about when to wake up. I always want to wake early; Kris always wants to sleep more. But it's too hot to move from 10.30 onwards and bad enough before. We settled for five. I've started giving her ten minutes of 'wake up' time so she can stir slowly. So ten to five I wake her and stand up and stretch just as a jeep comes charging towards us; the aqueduct is flatter than the dirt road. Close call.

California. What does that conjure up? Baywatch and Beverly Hills 90210. Valley girls and sunset strip. Blue-eyes, blond 'braided' hair, tanned legs, implanted breasts and surf-boards. I couldn't have been more wrong. Out here, this feels more like images of the deep south. Even the accents are broader. On our first day a cowboy on a horse came riding by—moccasins, Stetson, holsters, the lot. He even said "howdy" as he greeted us. (Did they put this on for the tourists? Is someone secretly arranging for film-extras to randomly ride the countryside to pass by the few non-American hikers in order to preserve an American myth?)

I've asked my friends and family to send me poems in an attempt to keep my brain ticking over as I walk. My father sent Ozymandias, King of Kings:

> *I met a traveller from an antique land*
> *Who said: Two vast and trunkless legs of stone*
> *Stand in the desert—near them on the sand,*
> *Half sunk, a shattered visage lies, whose frown,*
> *And wrinkled lip, and sneer of cold command,*
> *Tell that it's sculptured well—those passions read*

Which yet survive, stamped on those lifeless things,
The hand that mocked them and the heart that fed;
And on the pedestal these words appear;
"My name is Ozymandias, King of Kings:
Look on my works, ye Mighty and despair!"
Nothing beside remains. Round the decay
Of that colossal wreck, boundless and bare
The lone and level sands stretch far away.

*Ozymandias—*Shelley

It's not difficult to imagine coming across 'two vast and trunkless legs of stone' in this landscape. Only now we would be more likely to leave behind the vast and trunkless legs of a titanium space station, such as the one arbitrarily plonked in the landscape to my left. In centuries to come travellers will stumble across the 'United States'—a laptop half hidden in the sand on which is (or more likely, was) written:

The United States of America; Superpower:
Look on my works, ye Mighty and despair!

Archaeologists will come, analyse the remains of a rubbish dump, and surmise that the people of this land, rather foolishly, drank all of their water supply, chopped down all their trees, and polluted their air. How will they try to explain a society that went into self-destruct? Will they talk of 'live for the moment' concepts? Compare us to dinosaurs perhaps: "They grew too large," scientists will say. "They out-grew the food chain." Will they conjure up McDonald's out of the 'nothing that remains'? Be able to conceive of Wal-Mart in the 'boundless and bare' sands? Perhaps on the laptop there'll be a Coca-Cola ad—people in blue jeans dancing in a hot and dry landscape not unlike the one they find, drinking something which helps them to dehydrate even more quickly. Imagine how puzzled the historians will be, as they search the colossal wreck of a burnt-out four-wheel drive. Was this a suicidal nation? Or perhaps just a rather unsophisticated one?

Ok, so the guide book was right, it is hot and ugly. Just now we're hiding under the only cottonwood tree in Cottonwood Creek waiting for the wind to stir so that we can get battered rather than burnt. Joshua trees poke up from the tumbleweed like pom-pom girls in a horror movie.

Joshua tree

Anyone who has visited the States will remember having to answer the question 'Are you, or have you ever been, a member of the Communist Party?' Along with 'Have you ever been imprisoned, are you a terrorist, do you take hard drugs?' And then at the bottom of the form it says, 'If the answer to any of the above questions is yes, it does not necessarily preclude you from obtaining a visa.' Yeah, right. Well in keeping with more modern times (only ten years after the end of the Cold War), the question has changed to 'Do you have or have you ever had any connections to the Third Reich?' (!?)

This question floats in and out of my mind as we wander through rural redneck California where every other house flies a large American flag. (At first having seen one at the post office in Mount Laguna, I thought they were all post offices: "Look Kris, there's the post office! And another one! And another! . . .") People listen to Rush Limbaugh or Newt Gingrich on the radio. At one store we were talking about people who dump rubbish;

"They're not USA, they're Communist," said the store owner. Of the Amerindians I've heard, "Well, we won the war."

(What war? Who's we? Does that include me?)

"You carry protection?" everyone asks.

As if we would carry a gun when we've sent home our second plastic spoon and fork (now we have to take it in turns to eat). It does make one pause. You can't, if you run out of water, wander up to any old house or ranch. They have every right to shoot you after all. Every house has **BEWARE OF THE DOG** and **NO TRESPASSING** on the high-wired fence. The round/triangular PCT signs that indicate the trail are more often than not littered with bullet holes. Target practice. But then there are the kindly souls who leave out water on the trail, or yesterday—a cooler full of beer![8] And today some melon: gone sour, but it's the thought that counts.

This section sticks in mind as a haze of mad white windmills flapping, Joshua trees and panicking grasshoppers. At least 20 to 30 leap frantically into the air at each step and then charge haphazardly in all directions, crashing into you. Joshua trees were once the food for the giant ground sloth. They stand a head or two taller than the average human and have vicious spikes. They are our only source of shade and lunchtimes/siestas are spent following the strip of shadow around the tree as the sun moves. The guide book tells me they are actually members of the lily family, which is a difficult concept—I associate lilies with ponds and frogs and Monet. Joshua pointed out the route to Great Salt Lake for the Mormons, who were among the first western explorers here, and these tree-yuccas looked as if they were doing the same thing; hence the 'Joshua tree'.

The wind was so hard that you could hardly walk, buffeted sideways off the path (good place for the path to follow a ridge . . .). It was like being back in Edinburgh, flying off the top of Arthur's Seat, minus the rain. I can see why the windmills were a good idea. Environmentally friendly too. The San Gorgonio wind farm, along with the one at Tehachapi which we will pass in a few days, and another near San Francisco, produce thirty per cent of the world's entire wind-generated electricity and are among the largest wind farms in the world. The trail winds between the enormous white structures that rise up from the ground, and the horizon is a whirling haze of activity.

Now humbugs *are* actually hum-bugs. Who'd have thought it? There I was relaxing in a taught thin line under one of the above spiky sticks, when a small humming hovercraft swung by rather low in the sky, possibly having navigation/control difficulties due to the wind, and did a bit of a crash landing on to my sarong. It did cross my mind for a fleeting second that someone was lobbing the brown and white striped toffee-mints towards us in a friendly gesture (not all bad these youths of Lancaster/Palmdale). However, the bug/toffee-mint proceeded to bumble along, humming in a rather cheerful busy way.

Larry, Lily and Adrianna were all at the next trailhead (Tehachapi/Willow Springs Road) waiting—wonderful. Adrianna, an archaeologist, had busied herself and found an Amerindian site; some bits of tools made of chert lay scattered in the grass by the creek.

Mountains of Mexican food, ice cream, post office, groceries and then back to the trail where we collapsed by the water, camping next to a sign that said, 'No Loitering'.

Day 49—586.3 trail miles north
By a green gate

And a miserable day was had by all. Kris has decided that she can't make it to Canada and we've already been through the tearful discussion so only the misery and gloom are left. I remembered it was my birthday sometime mid-morning. Decided to sing a song.

> *Cope sent a letter frae Dunbar,*
> *Saying Charlie meet me an' ye daur,*
> *And I'll learn ye the art o' war,*
> *If you'll meet me i' the mornin'.*

> *Oh hey Johnnie Cope are ye waukin' yet?*
> *Or are your drums a beatin' yet?*
> *If ye are a waukin' I would wit,*
> *Tae gang tae the coals i' th' mornin'.*

It's a Scottish call to war. A marching song that keeps your feet pacing along. Rousing, at the very least.

It's like getting divorced and you have to decide within three days who gets what. Neither of us wants to separate. I want to get to Canada walking. She feels she can't. I want her to skip ahead, rest and wait for me. She wants me to stay with her and walk fewer miles a day.

Last night we were sitting by a stream in deep discussion over peanut butter crackers when some shots rang out above our heads. Teenagers, it turned out, out for a sporting night of shooting PCT signs.

And we're running out of food and today we ran out of fuel. So the pasta is at present sitting in water in the sun. We drink cold hot chocolate and cold tea already, so cold rehydrated pasta shouldn't be too hard to handle. Besides there's nothing else. Today, tomorrow and then half a Mars bar each for Tuesday. The plan is that I walk on ahead today, get up early tomorrow morning and walk the 15-odd miles left fast enough to get to Walker Pass for 10 a.m.—the time we told Adrianna and her family we would be there. Food. And then, if we're separating, we will have to buy new one-person bits of everything.

Now ants have arrived in uncountable quantities.

Took out *Words of Encouragement* and read the whole book in a gulp of self-pity and doubt. Not that encouraged. Time to 'go Jardine' on the book. Typical and quite refreshing that all the Brits say cold and hard things like:

> *Adversity is the first path to truth.* (Byron)
> *Success is going from failure to failure without loss of enthusiasm.* (Churchill)

The Americans say cheesy vacuous things. Here's one I like though, from Liza Minelli:

> *Reality is something you rise above.*

Not bad Liza.

I feel decidedly British. Everyone out here is super-friendly.

We are morose. The silence hurts and then there are huge tearful discussions.

Corn pasta. All hikers have strong opinions on corn pasta, I have found out. Never having tasted it in my life, I was quite open as to the results. Ray Jardine says it is fantastic for energy and that he and Jenny never tire of it. For variation he recommends having corn spaghetti every third meal instead of corn 'elbows'—not quite sure what these are exactly, I'm guessing macaroni. Other hikers talk about bringing it along for every meal (following Jardine's every word) and then having to dump it out at each stop, sick of the stuff. At the last stop, I persuaded Kris to take some out of the Hiker Box. Kris said she didn't like it much, but one meal would be ok. I said well, save us some money (free from the box), might as well try the stuff. Every meal since then it's been:

"Shall we have the corn pasta?"

"No, save it till tomorrow."

So now all we have left is corn pasta, our last meal, with no stove. You can't, as it turns out, rehydrate corn pasta. It disintegrates. So we had a yellow paste for lunch that resembled polyfiller that's been left just a minute too long and therefore has the odd congealed lump. It was worse than the semolina at primary school. And then there was powdered Parmesan and pesto to be spoon-fed. This is not good. This is not good at all.

Slept my first night alone—obviously bears were going to come. We've been following tracks for several days and Kris has the string to hang the food. What food? Well, the smell remains on everything. So stayed awake my first night alone waiting for them to come. We met a couple called Max and Robyn out here on the three-month plan a day ago, our first hikers since Christopher and Turtle left us at Agua Dulce. Max woke up one night last week to find a bear sniffing the back of his neck. Bears are big. Very big. Can climb trees and rip their way through cars to get food.

Day 53—647.8 trail miles north
Walker Pass

They didn't come (the bears) and I made it down the mountain for ten o'clock. Too hungry/sick to eat the crackers I had left over. No water at the campsite. So I *ate* a packet of Emergen-C Cranberry powdered juice mix. According to the packet it has 38 active mineral complexes. Can't handle any more complexes just now.

There was a note from Christopher in the register from 17th June. *Happy Birthday Natasha*, it said. How nice of him.

And then the sweet sound of Adrianna's voice. Food. Adrianna, Lily, Larry, Ghengis and Bentley (the last two are dogs) had driven all the way from Lancaster to meet us. Food glorious food.

"You wanna hear how we met?" asks Larry as we drive along in the car. "She sued me!" he said, still outraged after 40 years of marriage, "She god-damn sued me!!"

Lillian was the make-up artist on one of Larry's sequels which was filmed in Hawaii. The first night there, the crew and actors who had all worked on the first production went out for a drink or two. Lillian woke up at 5 a.m., ready to start making-up at 6 a.m. as scheduled. No-one emerged until rather late in the morning. She said nothing, worked her hours and then carried on working, marking the extra hours down as overtime. The second day was the same story.

"No-one showed, honey, not one person," she chips in to Larry's story, turning her whole body round to tell me in the back seat. She said nothing, put in the overtime. Day three and so on, Lily rising and ready by six each day, no-one appearing until midday, sometimes not even until later. At the end of the shoot she presented Larry with a bill.

"Hell woman! I'm not paying that!" said Larry, probably with a whole heap more expletives. ("You can't stop us cussin'," says Adrianna.)

"And then she sued me! God-damn sued me."

"And I won too," chips in Lily with a decisive nod.

"Had to marry her, took me for every penny I had, sure as hell bankrupted me, had to god-damn marry her," laughs Larry grinning from ear to ear.

We took some food back to Walker Pass and picked up Kris. We are going to the 'quaint' (guide book) town of Kernville to stay at a motel and sort things out. Honeymoon and divorce in one.

Long, long discussions with the support crew back home. More "But you said . . ." and "I don't want . . ." this time without a hoard of termites trying to take Kris's pack away in the belief that it was a dead animal. Finally friendship wins through. Kind of.

So, we're going together to Kennedy Meadows. Then if the snow is bad Kris will jump ahead and I will catch her up. If it's not we will both continue walking at our different paces and I will try to jump ahead to Washington to a place in the middle of nowhere on the Canadian border and then come back and we can walk through Oregon together. We have talked round and round the options.

Kris does not want to miss any more miles. She regrets the

ones she missed around Wrightwood. She knows she's not going to walk the whole trail, but wants to walk the whole of California at least and not to skip sections. Uncompromising.

I know I can do it. Still. I can get to Canada. And while there's still a chance I do not want to give up this dream. Uncompromising.

I'm trying to be fair here. Trying to write it as it was. But my truth will never be Kris's truth. (Is it me or is she being completely unreasonable? It's easy Kris, it's black and white! Either you have a serious injury and it hurts in which case you stop walking, or you don't, in which case you stop complaining and cheer up. But it all feels very grey.)

We are tired.

We left our motel room and came back to Walker Pass. Hiked two miles up into the mountains where Kris finally succumbed to 650 miles of pain from walking on a strained tendon and decided to rest for a few weeks. We ate my birthday chocolate mousse cake. Or ate the two spoonfuls we could manage each. Then came back down in the morning. Hitched to Onyx where forlornly we parted; she, taking a bus to Lake Isabella, then Bakersfield, then northbound for Canada; I, back to stand on the side of the road to do what I have always considered stupid in the extreme and hitch alone back to Walker Pass. All this talk, two months of "will we make it or not?" are reduced to a brief exchange of items. I have been carrying more and more to make Kris's load lighter and from Tehachapi have taken almost all the food. My shoulders crunch and my back aches. I abandon things without thought. Tarp? I hate it, got to go. Tent? (Which we have only just picked up from the post office), too heavy—go. Got this far on building wrap, how much more does one need? I'll be fine.

Walking has always been my method of shifting emotions. Which is a good thing as there's nothing else to do but walk. I walk. And think of Kris on a bus. She will come back to meet me further north.

CENTRAL CALIFORNIA

BEAR

Day 56—659.3 trail miles north
Joshua Tree Spring

So I'm sitting by a spring, having eaten my ration of peanut butter, and am tapping away on the pocketmail. ('Pocketmail' is how we communicate. It's a pencilcase-size machine with a tiny keyboard. In town we can hold it up to a telephone and it makes noises like a fax machine, sending and receiving emails.) So there I am trying to squeeze my fingers into touch-typing on this very small pad. Actually I'm writing to Charles. Charles of the everybody-needs-a-Charles day. Well why not, what have I got to lose? He's single; he runs marathons and he's generous and well, sexy. Perhaps he'll follow me across America meeting me at each town-stop with fresh fruit and yoghurt? Ok perhaps not, but it's worth a try, he might just be persuaded to come and visit me on the July 4th holiday weekend. So I'm ensconced in the delicate art of flirting by email—can't be too subtle, he's American after all—sucking on a spoon of peanut butter in between thought, and airing my toes and occasionally glancing over at the peanut butter jar to check the ants haven't arrived and ohmygod it's a bear! *IT'S A BEAR! It's a large brown bear. A bear . . . I'm . . . it's . . . I . . . drinking from the spring not ten feet away, a bear. I'm sitting down with no shoes and socks on, holding a jar of peanut butter, and there's a bear—right there. Ok it's gone. God my heart is going like one of those incessant woodpeckers. A bear! Oh my God, I just saw a bear. Aah! it's back. It's back. Other side of stream. Ok I'm going, got to get photos . . . .*

So I grabbed my camera and crept around the corner after it, still barefoot. I turned the corner and started snapping. It crossed the creek and started meandering towards me. It wasn't *that* big, I mean big, but not quite as big as you'd think, not as big as imagined, unless—a baby bear? . . . and the warning signals went off in my head: somewhere around is mother bear! So I opened my mouth and made some whooshing noises, feebly attempting to scare it away, but my voice was stuck in my throat—a mouse would not even have turned a hair. The bear keeps on coming. I step sideways and a rattlesnake starts up, coiled at the bottom of the tree beside me. Both bear and I beat a hasty retreat.

I saw a bear! I SAW A BEAR!

That __ was __ amazing. That was incredible. That was wonderful. That was terrifying but so exhilarating. I saw a bear, in the wilderness, that close to me, I saw a BEAR!!!! Wahoooo!!!!

Ok, time to think now.

Must hang my food tonight: 15 feet off the ground, six feet away from the tree trunk, on a branch that's strong enough to take the weight of the food, but not the weight of a bear. Hanging includes everything that might smell, like toothpaste and moisturiser as well as food. Kris showed me how to do it and after a few attempts it's successfully hanging high and happy in the tree. Satisfied, I turned to unpack the rest of my belongings for the night.

"Bear'll get that, easy," says a voice. "Just pull the string and it'll come down the other side."

I look back up at the yellow string bag hanging in the tree. Annoyingly he's right.

"What you gotta do is . . . ," and he explained the balancing method to me, where you pull one bag up high into the tree and then attach a second bag which is light enough to go up to meet the first bag but not so light as to go over the top. It's important to remember to have some string hanging down to retrieve the bag in the morning. I only have one food bag. And it sounds complicated.

"Would you like to, err, hang together?" I ask.

"Oh no," says the hiker, "I never hang my food. Just sleep with it, right by my head inside my tent. That way I can hear the bears if they come."

I felt like mentioning that he wouldn't be hearing anything for too much longer once the bear had taken a swipe at his food and sliced through his head by mistake. Foolish as it may seem, this lack of concern turned out not to be uncommon on the PCT—there were more people who didn't hang than who did. To them the likelihood of being attacked by a bear was remote, whereas the likelihood of a bear stealing their food was great. And you don't take food from a thru-hiker.

"Oh!" said I, somewhat contritely, "Well, there is a bear."

He looked at me.

"Here." I said.

He looked even more unconvinced.

"There," I said, and pointed up the hill to the bear which was now snuffling the ground in search of acorns about 20 yards away.

He looked at the bear, gave a few manly shouts and snuck off to get his camera. The bear meanwhile has taken no interest in any of our antics or our food. Just for good measure, I threw a few stones in its direction. It ignored the first few and then suddenly leapt playfully up a tree. If bears can laugh, then this bear is definitely laughing.

Black Bear at Joshua Tree Spring

I almost killed a rattlesnake last week by throwing stones, not, I hasten to add, intentionally. It was curled up on the trail and I was trying to get it to move off the trail. One stone lopped on to its head then the rattle went: "**RRR-rrrrrrrr**-rrrrr-rrr-rr-r-r- . . . ." like a toy running out of batteries. It had recovered sufficiently to give a healthy "rrrr" when Kris passed it later. I don't think there's the slightest chance of injuring a bear this way. Those who 'went west' reported shooting whole rounds into Grizzlies who just kept walking on towards their victims, barely noticing the bullets. Also I have no intention of annoying what would appear to be a happy hungry bear.

I untied my string and wound it round the bag and then re-tied it around the trunk of the tree.

"Still get that," said Gene, who had returned with his camera.

Gene is a veteran of many things; war, long-distance hiking, raising money for charity, and even CIA recruitment. Gene is also hoping to make it to Canada. He is carrying a large plastic jar which he fills with pasta and rice and then water and rehydrates his food. He eats cold and has no stove. He knows he is late but reckons he walks fast enough to make it. He has done the Appalachian Trail and knows what's what. A few days ahead are another couple who Kris and I met before Walker Pass, Max and Robyn, but they walk fast, very fast and they only have three months off work. Christopher and Turtle must be almost a week ahead by now. Can I catch them up? It's 57 days since we started. 659.3 miles. 2000 miles to go. June 25th. Three months or less of ok weather left.

I walk well, enjoying my own regime. Charging up the hills, testing my fitness, pushing my body. I am alone. Just me and the mountains and this barely suppressible sense of excitement; I am doing this. My legs have a bounce—muscles that are enjoying and meeting the challenge. The air is good, the air is fantastic; crisp and so fresh, and all around me the chickadees flit from branch to branch, whilst the tree-creepers casually stand at right-angles on the tree trunks and hop downwards with an irreverent nod to gravity, like abseilers going face first. I discovered a strange red plant and, fascinated, I spent ages photographing it. I later found out it was a snowplant—a parasite which lives off the roots of pine trees.

It is Sunday. A beautiful sunny Sunday. And that's when I reach my first real river, the South Fork Kern River, a good three foot deep and at least twelve-foot wide. The clear water is singing, the grass is green, the mountains white, the dragonflies flit from rock to rock:—this is surely the picture of paradise that hikers are hoping for when they set off into the wilderness. Who needs love when there is this? Who needs a man when I've seen a bear! This is why I came. I'm happy. Hah!

Finally arrived at the much talked about Kennedy Meadows, but sadly no Meadow Ed. He'd gone north a week before, to follow the hikers. Am I really so late? Kennedy Meadows is basically a store and 12 residents. They got a telephone line last year, after a legal fight with the telephone company. The store holds packets for hikers and this is the start of the real (as opposed to the official) Sierra. Rivers deep enough to swim in and sometimes strong enough to make crossing them dangerous. Snow. Mountains. Real mountains. I can't wait. At the store my parcels await me—food for two people, crampons, ice axes, gloves, coats, winter-gear. The word on the ground is that the snow is not bad so I sent everything back with glee. My pack is still too heavy. Stove? What do I need a stove for? The stove is the next heavy item in my pack. I can rehydrate like Gene does. I keep my Gore-Tex jacket in a moment of rationality. No gloves, no tent, no trousers (legs can walk to get warm, can't they?), no stove, no crampons, no ice axe and considerably less food; juice mix? Don't like it; don't need it. Nuts and seeds? Don't like 'em, don't need 'em. Sweets? Don't like 'em, don't need 'em. Sugar and salt? Don't like 'em, don't need 'em. Crackers? Don't like 'em, don't need 'em. I've gained weight after all. I keep the hot chocolate, the powdered milk, the granola, the pasta and the much loved Kris-spaghetti sauce leather which just tantalises my appetite for vegetables, the dried fruit, the Mars bars and the peanut butter. My pack weighs less on leaving Kennedy Meadows than it did arriving. This is very good.

The first clouds, the first grass—green grass, rivers with water, and finally mountains. Mount Whitney, California's highest mountain at 14,492 feet, pokes up above Monache Meadows.

ON TOP OF THE WORLD

Day 60—738.2 trail miles north
Mulkey Pass

Of course the first night out it was freezing. Literally. My blue sleeping bag was white with frost; the building wrap had frozen to the ground. Hot coffee? Hot tea? Or cold chocolate . . . . The drinking hose to my water bag had completely frozen, the bag itself was half way there. I munched through a breakfast of grape nuts and ice chips. Gloves would definitely have been handy. Trousers would be . . . . It doesn't bear thinking about. I did what you're not supposed to do and ate inside my sleeping bag—a bear may take a swipe at me further down the track, but best to save from freezing to death now. Sun, rise up and save me!

Here in the mountains the chipmunks are scurrying around, the marmots are poking their heads out curiously from fallen trees and the birds are chirruping. In the morning I was attacked by a bird—a large jay dive-bombed me shrieking away at the top of its voice. It had me running along the trail with my pack lopping up and down. You would have thought it would be used to hikers by now. According to Amerindian legend, the Sierra Nevada was created out of a competition between Hawk and Crow who piled up mud from the big lake that was here before. Hawks, ravens, eagles and the great grey owl have all been spotted along with many smaller birds including the red-breasted nuthatch, dusky flycatcher, Williamson's sapsucker, and woodpeckers, blue jays and chickadees in their hundreds. I also saw a western tanager the other day—a bright yellow bird whose head turns red in the mating season. I am collecting the odd stray feathers left on the ground—beautiful orange/pink ones with black tips, or tiny fluffy white yellow and black centimetre-long specks of feather.

The trail has wound its way up through meadows and large boulders, through forests of pinyon pines which grow out of the gravelly dust, through slabs of granite and by wide meandering rivers. It is the very perfection of heaven. One can imagine the joy and exhilaration of those first white visitors as they and their horses dragged their few possessions up through the trees and springs to suddenly arrive at the green expanse of Monache Meadow with its backdrop of stone mountains. Imagine coming from the grime of wet cold industrial London to this paradise. This is perhaps the most remote of all the wildernesses I will walk through. One hundred and fifty airline miles of land uncrossed by a road, from Walker Pass to Tuolumne Meadows in Yosemite. The Sierra Nevada. It is also one of the hardest sections of the trail in which to re-supply, as there are no nearby settlements. From Lone Pine (itself a three and a half mile hike off-trail plus a 23 mile hitchhike) I am aiming to go all the way to Vermilion Valley which is roughly 130 miles. I am giving myself eight days in which to do this which is about 17-18 miles a day. Eight days of food weighs a considerable amount. The guide book tells me that if I get hungry—in the autumn—I can always resort to the nuts of the pinyon pines. That's if I have the patience and the resourcefulness to gather the pine cones and heat them at a low temperature in an oven until they open. This is unlikely to happen, even if it were the right season. The Kawaiisu people used to grind these nuts to make flour and many still collect them today.

I passed through a semi-burnt forest of pinyon pines today. The trunks of the trees had twisted their shades of orange and brown into spectacular sculpted formations. I dropped my pack and lay down in the sand to get the best angle on each exhibit. The trees really are amazing here. Adrianna took us to see one of the ancient sequoias in the Sequoia National Park. It was an enormous redwood with a whole room at the opening of its base. There are redwoods that grow so large, I am told, that you can drive a car through them. Unfortunately only a few such incredible specimens remain and most of the sequoias that we walk by are all new growth—mere infants in the tree cycle. The Mono people named these trees 'woh-woh-nau', after their guardian spirit, the owl. The owl, it is said, will bring evil on those who cut down the big trees.

Neither the pinyon pines nor the sequoias make good bear-hanging trees. They are either too short and scrubby or have too many branches. Presuming that there is a suitable tree, it takes me a good ten minutes each night just to throw the string over the branch. I tie one end to a stone and then hurl the stone upwards but my throwing skills aren't particularly good. Arms are getting weaker, legs stronger. My back is now reduced to skin and bones, so much so that the pack now rubs on the bones of my shoulders. Time to employ my old flatmate's tip for uses of thick hiking socks as padding. Legs on the other hand—my thighs don't touch in the middle and yet are huge powerful things.

My feet have holes in them. It's not that they hurt. It's not that they smell. It's not that the skin is peeling, so it wouldn't appear to be athlete's foot (not that I've ever had athlete's foot before, but I have a vague idea that they are the symptoms). They just have holes—my soles looks like the surface of the moon, cratered. Very strange.

At Cottonwood Pass I met Max and Robyn on the way up from Lone Pine who told me that Meadow Ed was waiting at the bottom for 'the girls' i.e. Kris and myself. News travels quickly from north to south, but slowly or not at all from south to north. Anyway I was delighted to see them and, with the thought of seeing Meadow Ed, I skipped down the mountain. Also Kris's sister had sent me a bivvy (a sort of water-proof sleeping bag with a slightly raised tent bit at the head end) to Lone Pine which would make the nights a bit more cosy and perhaps less scary. At the bottom there was no Meadow Ed however. Had he gone up Trail Pass Trail to meet us there? Not just no Meadow Ed, but no-one at all. And it was 23 miles into town. After several hours two people emerged from the mountains and I begged a lift, bouncing around in the boot of a two-seater with two large and unpleasant mastiffs as we zigzagged down into the trough of the dry dusty plains.

Lone Pine. First things first—find a telephone to send and receive emails: Charles is coming. The man-who-everybody-needs is on his way here already, in fact, to Lone Pine. I have a 'date'! The only problem being that the last time I showered was on June 23rd, which was five days ago, the last time I washed my clothes was on June 22nd, and the last time I washed my hair was in April. Not exactly 'date' conditions.

I started wandering vaguely around the 'two-pine town' with a vain hope of finding a public shower or, failing that, a fire-station, where they might with some pleading permit a hiker to douse herself under the hose at least. Then I bumped into Matt, the investment banker, who I had last seen at Anza. He looked very un-bank like with a healthy growth of stubble, a fishing rod and a guitar. He had given up on hiking the trail and was hitching up and down the Sierras, hiking the most scenic bits, stopping to fish and strum every now and then. Matt solved the problem by suggesting that we spend the afternoon in *Jake's Saloon* drinking 'Jake's hard lemonade', and I let my apprehension lessen somewhat. A date!

Day 65—743.8 trail miles north
Cottonwood Pass

Charles was nice, he was pleasant, and oh so very charming. I got to shower in a motel (luxury!) and even soak in a spa, which was incredible, and we wined and dined. He also, rather usefully, was able to recommend zinc oxide to cure my holey-heel problem.

By Friday the bivvy had still not turned up and I thought, "Ahch, what the hell" and Charles drove me to Los Angeles for the weekend. I need a break: more baths, more carpets and more nephew. On Monday, my brother brought me back to Lone Pine, and this time I bumped into a rather forlorn Bald Eagle and Nocona. Nocona had altitude problems and they had had to stop walking. So instead they had hired a car and were on their way to see Death Valley. Still no bivvy, oh well, so I hitched up to Horseshoe Meadows, first with Jack, Harry and Bob—a sort of wealthy version of the characters of *Last of the Summer Wine*—who were on their way to fly gliders, and then with a rookie ranger who was spending the summer in Monache Meadows and had come down to re-supply. Then a three and a half mile hike back up 350-odd metres to the trail at 11,160 feet, then an hour or so's stone-throwing, and finally sleep.

Day 67—760.5 trail miles north
Crabtree Meadows

The first person to summit Mt. Whitney (14,494 feet) on this cold day. Stunning views out over the Sierra—blue lakes, stone mountains: the first real views of the trip.

Mount Whitney summit—14,494 feet

I left my pack by Guitar Lake and built a small anti-marmot fortress around my food as it was above the tree line and then, suddenly weighing 30-odd pounds less, I practically ran up the mountain, exhilarated with feeling so light and healthy. Not far from the top the trail joins the Whitney Portal Trail which ascends from Lone Pine. And it is up this route that the tourists come one by one, a steady stream throughout the summer. There is also a rather terrifying notice at this trail intersection which reads as follows:

EXTREME DANGER FROM LIGHTNING

**TO AVOID BEING STRUCK BY LIGHTNING,
IMMEDIATELY LEAVE THE AREA IF ANY
OF THE FOLLOWING CONDITIONS EXIST.**

- DARK CLOUDS NEARBY
- THUNDER, HAIL, OR RAIN
- HISSING IN THE AIR
- STATIC ELECTRICITY
IN THE HAIR OR THE FINGERTIPS

**THE WHITNEY SHELTER WILL NOT
OFFER PROTECTION. YOU SHOULD LEAVE
THE SUMMIT AND PROCEED TO A LOWER
ELEVATION.**

Every day the storm clouds build up from about mid-day onwards—large, perfectly shaped textbook *cumuli nimbus* clouds or mushrooms in an otherwise empty sky. So far I have (just) managed to avoid the storm that then breaks each afternoon.

It was so cold at the top that the run down after the initial slow descent through the snow at the peak, was almost a necessity. Back at the mesmerising Guitar Lake, the marmots had been laying siege to my fortress. Thankfully the food was still all there—re-supplying now would mean going back up Whitney and then 30-odd miles down the other side, and *then* back up again with all the food, not a nice thought. Determined to eat something, they had chewed through my sleeping-mat and spat out little blue chips everywhere. Grateful not to have lost more, I came down to Crabtree Meadows and decided not to move on. (Losing the drive? But then yesterday was over 20 miles.) It's a beautiful spot. Here the straw-hat threesome who took the holiday and went home for a week to lie on the beach came flying by. I declined their offer to walk with them and stopped just to enjoy. An ex-drummer turned printer from Bournemouth and a record company executive from

'LaLaLand' out for the weekend to climb Whitney are here to keep me company and feed me hot liquid. Campfire, Southern Comfort—and early in the morning the deer go by not 15 feet away with their big round teddy-bear ears. I am happy. Ridiculously happy.

Life is good, life is promising. I wander along daydreaming. Will I fall in love? Perhaps I'll end up moving to Hollywood and starring in a movie. Or perhaps we'll live in New York and I'll write editorials for the *New York Times*. Ok, perhaps not. But it's amazing how quickly the time passes wandering along ensconced in these dreams of maybes and might-bes and all the time surrounded by silent mountains and raging water. Here anything seems possible and yet at the same time you are reminded just how transient you are. I can be everything, but that everything will always be so little.

It took me over an hour to hang my food last night. First I just couldn't get the stone over the branch. Then the stone went flying over leaving the string behind. Then stone number nine landed perfectly balanced on the branch which would have been incredible had I been aiming to do that, as the branch was really only as wide as the stone. In attempting to dislodge the stone I managed to get both ends of the string tangled in various branches and only with luck and the aid of a long stick did I re-acquire my rope. After this performance, stone number eleven finally came through.

The trick is getting the right stone—light enough to be throwable, heavy enough to pull the string down the other side. Fatal error: not holding on to the other end of the string. So I ate beneath my rope, away from my camping spot, hurriedly, as it was getting dark. Then came the real crunch. Food tends to weigh a lot, even dehydrated dried food. What happens is it gets to just above your head and then won't move. The more you pull, the more the string threatens to snap where it goes over the branch. I tried poking it up with a stick. I tried emptying out half and loading half into the air to put the other half on as a counter-balance. But to no avail. Eventually, now in the dark, the little grey cells clicked and I re-tied the bag, leaving some string with a loop. I put the pulling string through the loop, lifted the bag as high as I could and then levered it outwards and upwards with the aid of a foxtail pine. A bear could probably still have got it somehow.

The trail climbs up and up past ice-cold lakes and into barren glaciated bowls. Occasionally a clump of blue or purple flowers peaks out from behind a rock, but there is little vegetation and a surprising number of yellow-bellied marmots. Each time the trail heads straight towards a stone cliff-face that couldn't possibly house a bird's nest let alone a well-gradiated path. And yet each time the trail zigzags up the cliff-face to some notch between the huge mountains where the wind howls through. Up to the highest point on the PCT: Forester Pass, 13,200 feet. Hard work. And then down the other side where the snow was definitely not ice-axe worthy but made for a scary descent all the same. I lost the path at one point and had to scramble back up over boulders and scree. Stunning views. Finally the route has arrived at something spectacular. And then a plunge down into the Kings Canyon Wilderness with the Kearsarge Pinnacles jaggedly poking out on one side.

At the bottom in Vidette Meadows I finally stopped (21 miles) at 5.30 in the evening and was instantly plagued by hoards of mosquitoes. These bug nets were an essential buy. Then an hour later and they are all gone. Another campfire, though it's not quite as cold as last night. Or the night before that which was perishing.

The PCT has now joined the John Muir Trail and is busy with people. The JMT goes from Yosemite to Whitney (220 odd miles) and is therefore the perfect hiking holiday length, though I imagine that it's only on the last day that the pain from blisters, muscles and back abates enough to enjoy the walking. It is nice to meet people going in the other direction though still a little surprising when they greet you with: "So you're raising money for Oxfam?" News travels fast on the hiker highway. I am walking alone; I seem to be the last PCT thru-hiker. But every day I hear news of other hikers maybe a day, two days ahead. Gene, who overtook me when I went to Lone Pine and Los Angeles? Max and Robyn? Straw-hat people? I am walking much faster than I expected. Doing more miles. If I can keep this up, I have a good chance of getting to

Canada still. Although this seems to matter less and less—the exhilaration of walking and climbing, of feeling this strong, of the scenery, is enough.

Time to crawl into bed and hope the whine of the mosquitoes (out again now—a different variety?) doesn't keep me awake.

Day 70—828.8 trail miles north
Grouse Meadows

Left Vidette Meadow at 6.30 a.m. to struggle slowly up 2400 feet to Glen Pass. Then a rocky trail and snow patches made the descent even slower and wearing on the knees and ankles. When the trail finally evened out by the beautiful Rae Lakes, the mosquitoes made enjoying the view impossible. My Mars bar break turned into a leg-slapping Greek-style dance and I decided after that not to stop whatever the aches and pains. Down to 8,492 feet and then a hot climb, trying to kill the evil things that were biting through the net, up to Pinchot Pass at 12,130 feet. Poor Pinchot, Chief of Forestry under Roosevelt, was sacked for revealing that the Secretary of the Interior, Richard A. Ballinger, had given parts of Alaska to friends who had already agreed to sell the land to a mining syndicate.

Ran down the other side as darkness came on rapidly and found two ex-Scouts with their ex-Scout master camped by Lake Marjorie; they fed me hot tea and thankfully offered the spare space in their bear-containers. (These are specially designed rotund containers which the less experienced bear has difficulties in opening. They are too heavy for most thru-hikers to consider carrying.) It would have been at least another two miles to the next tree and I'd done twenty-three already. Tired, but satisfied. Pleased.

Today was another pass and then down the 'Golden Staircase' which is the knee-crippling path through the Palisade Gorge. Here at the bottom there are only one or two mosquitoes, so strip-off-and-plunge-in time. Ice cold water, beautifully refreshing.

This is good. This is all so good. I am walking from Mexico to

Canada, through the wilderness, at one with nature. Oh you can laugh at the cheesy lines, but there's usually truth in clichés. Your body and mind adapt surprisingly quickly, develop skills you never knew you had, become comfortable with all sorts of unknowns. My mind is so attuned to walking north, that as soon as the trail veers overtly east or west, little alarm bells go off in my head. I sent my compass on to Washington. It has been sunny every day and the trail is clear if not well marked; there seems little likelihood of getting lost. I still look for footprints that I might recognise (like Turtle's or Christopher's) but here in the Sierras there is a steady flow of hikers going in all directions that cover up the thru-hiker tracks. Beautiful. The world is beautiful.

BUGS, BEARS, AND ANOTHER CREEK

Day 72—864.9 trail miles north
Hilgard Creek

Why am I doing this? This is hell. This is grim. This is not an enjoyable hobby or pastime. This is an endurance test. I'm lying wrapped in the building-wrap, Gore-Tex jacket on, head, hands and journal all inside the mosquito net, terrified that they can get to my feet, waiting for rain.

I met three hearty southerners with their fishing rods on the way down from the low-ish Seldon Pass (a mere 10,900 feet).

"It doesn't get worse than this does it?" I asked, unable to imagine anything beyond what had already been. Lunch at the top of the pass was spent wrapped in the same cocoon; eating is almost becoming too horrible to bother with.

"No, no this is the worst. There's nothing worse than this."

Then it began to drizzle and instantly it was 10,000 times worse. 10,000 mosquitoes worse.

I seem to be lying on an ant's nest. They'll have to move; I can't. God I miss the chaparral and the desert. Give me ants rather than mosquitoes any day.

The only thing to do is to keep moving at all costs whilst trying to slap the back of your knees. My expensive Gore-Tex jacket which everyone has been trying to make me send home ("too heavy", "not needed") has become a haven, not from the rain, but from the bugs. It's one of the few things they can't bite through. Then horror of horrors, a ford. Dropped the pack, grabbed the flip-flops and ran (they swarm around the pack for about two seconds). Took off the boots and socks whilst ten million of the things turned my legs black. Grabbed the pack and charged into the river where you cannot be bitten under water. Yesterday it was the same hell for the crossing of dangerous Evolution Creek. The bugs were so bad that I threw myself in totally forgetting current and river crossing techniques, just grateful to have water up to the thighs. Halfway across and I realised it was actually getting quite deep. My sleeping bag was packed at the bottom of my pack, and it would be a bad move to get that wet. Held the camera up, trying to walk slowly and evenly, steadily against the pressure of the current, and not listen to the panic and irritation of the thick cloud of biting insects attacking everywhere. I breathed in and kept going, vaguely noticing someone hailing me from the other side who I completely ignored, and got across, mostly dry. The hiker was Gene, now re-christened 'Flatfoot', last seen before the turn off to Lone Pine at Cottonwood Pass. He was anxious to hear my news.

"You must have walked like the wind!" he said.

"Can't stop!" I gasped, hammering my boots back on to wet feet. "Legs, no trousers, mosquitoes."

He nodded, "Deet?" he asked.

"No Deet, no trousers, got to go, can't stop."

It's been like that for four days now. I'm exhausted. Right now, I can't unpack and crawl into the safety of my sleeping bag because it is thundering. If it rains the only thing to do is walk.

A tent! A tent! My kingdom for a tent!

Though a horse wouldn't be all that bad just now.

So I've done (I think) most of the dangerous bits—Muir Pass was several miles of deep snow. Lots of clambering up on to high rocks to find the trail and then cutting steps into the mountain. Slow walking but good, challenging, and at least there were no mosquitoes up there; although the insides of my calves are scraped raw from the 'post'-holes in the snow (yes, trousers might have been handy). Either side of the pass lies a beautiful lake—one named Helen and the other Wanda after the daughters of John Muir. Both lakes were covered in drifting clumps of ice and glowed a lovely pale blue. John Muir was a Scot from Dunbar who emigrated to the States aged 11. At the age of 30 he explored the Sierra Nevada, which he re-christened the 'Range of Light', and fell in love with the mountains. Carrying a loaf of bread and travelling with only an overcoat he used to just get up and walk if it got too cold at night. He was also instrumental in the setting up of the National Park system in the U.S.A. and started the Sierra Club to help protect Yosemite and the Sierra Nevada from the cattle ranchers and others. He died in 1914, an inspirational figure and a fantastic mountaineer.

Obviously I'm not quite as hardy as he was—it's true, I have no stove and no tent and no trousers, but I don't think I would make that a lifetime's hiking decision. I have, at least, finally worked out how to eat without making mosquito-sandwich the fare of each meal and getting my face and hands drained of blood in return. I eat inside the bug-shirt, the same way as I'm writing now. A bit messy and not great for bears (the smell will stay on the clothes and I also sleep in it) but definitely an improvement. I don't care. I know I should care, but I don't. Kris would care. But right now the bugs are so tortuous that a bear seems preferable.

Took a ferry from the middle of nowhere to the middle of slightly less nowhere, across Lake Edison to Vermilion Valley Resort, where Gene (Flatfoot) popped up again, this time following me, and we discovered another PCT hiker, Hobbit, as well as an array of people hiking the John Muir Trail. At Vermilion Valley they receive post once a week and hold packages for hikers—a vital food stop for the northbound PCT hiker and an enjoyable one for the JMT hikers. Hospitality flowed as did the food (fantastic fruit pies) and the hiker stories.

"Met a guy on the AT who carried his cat. Curled up on top of the pack, caught 20-odd mice each night."

The AT (Appalachian Trail) has shelters which apparently sleep more mice than hikers. One has an infamous resident rat the size of a cat.

At the trail junction at Kearsarge Pass—a trail which descends nine miles down into Onion Valley where you can hitchhike another 15 miles to the town of Independence—one hiker came across a fellow jogging along in a T-shirt, shorts and a baseball cap, with a ghetto-blaster on his shoulder and nothing else. The guy was trying to get from one side of the Sierras (Independence) to the other (Fresno). Rather than trying to hitch all the way round the bottom of the mountains, he looked at a road map and thought 'I'll just nip across that way.' The road map has little indication of what exactly you would have to cross, and so there he was, running across the mountains, taking the most direct route. Let's hope he made it.

And then, as we get closer and closer to Yosemite, the bear scare stories magnify daily. One JMT-er, Tony, who incidentally offered to fly (fly!?) me a tent from his home in Monterey Bay, hung his food with another hiker. They tied their two ropes to the bags and flung each end over a different tree then hoisted them both up leaving the bags suspended 20 feet up, ten feet from the nearest branch. Foolproof. A bear came to the camp, walked round them, walked straight past them up to where the food was hanging. They followed and by the time they got there the food was on the floor. It left the teabags.

Or there's the one about the Girl Scout who was wandering merrily down the trail with her troupe when a bear came out of the woods and grabbed her pack off her back and disappeared back into the woods.

Or the one about the AT hiker, Fearless (on the PCT this year), who woke up to piteous cries of "Help, help!" He crawled out of his tent to see his companion's tent disappearing down the hillside with the companion still inside it. The bear it seems couldn't be bothered with ripping the tent open, just thought he'd use the whole thing as a sack. Another Scout was actually killed this way in Yosemite this year—there was no Fearless to help get him out of the tent and his head hit a rock as the bear dragged the tent away.

To this end I am purposely keeping my mileage down so that I can camp before Donohue Pass (the start of Lyell Valley) and make it in one day to Tuolumne Meadows. Lyell Valley is otherwise known as 'Bear Alley'.

Day 75—903.6 trail miles north
Minaret Falls

Did a wee detour tourist trip to visit the Devil's Postpile—a strange volcanic rock formation—and to nip into the heavenly hot-spring showers in Reds Meadows. At the top of the Postpile the large beams of lava have been smoothed by glacial activity into smooth hexagon-shaped tiles. That night a deer came up a hill and arrived abruptly upon me, much to its surprise. It stood and gawped at me just a few feet away. And earlier in the evening I saw a marten, at least I think it was a marten. It looked like an elongated red squirrel with a slightly pointier face and its body bunched up when it moved, like a caterpillar.

Postpile

Better to cross Minaret Falls last thing at night or first thing in the morning? Morning definitely. You can walk all day with wet feet, they'll dry off, but going to bed with wet feet and having to put wet shoes and socks on the next morning? Not nice and not a good idea. So early the next morning there was the beautiful wide tumble of Minaret Falls, and with quite a lot of hop, skip and jumping, it was actually possible to get from grass clump to log to grass clump, and not even get wet feet. Then it was back across the San Joaquin River and a steady climb up to the top of the gorge. The valley is a massive and very steep V. On the west side the John Muir Trail dips in and out, up and down, gully and knoll, weaving and winding, dropping and climbing, struggling on the slopes of the Ritter Range. Theirs is the strenuous route as the PCT climbs its very gentle gradient slowly upwards in one long day and gets the views. We are going up, up to the next big pass. From the PCT you can gaze across the valley to the other side and see the perfect dark blue of Shadow Lake placed neatly and smoothly inside the rugged grey granite, never seeing the sun. Downstream from here are the fruit farms that gave California its status as the land of plenty, the land of promise. It was to the San Joaquin valley that the 'Okies' came in the 1930s and 1940s, as depicted in John Steinbeck's *The Grapes of Wrath*. Not strictly from Oklahoma, the Okies were crop-sharers, farmers and white-collar workers forced to seek a living elsewhere after the devastating dust-bowl storms that swept across the cotton belt of Oklahoma, Arkansas, Texas and Missouri. They came, largely white and protestant, as whole families piled into high cars that were their homes. They came, some 80,000 desperate people, expecting employment and quick money and found they had to compete, much to the disgust of many, with hispanics and asians already on the fruit-picking circuits. They were quickly labelled as hillbillies. Many stayed, adding to California's conundrum of origins.

Nowadays, this section of the San Joaquin at least is flourishing with tourists. Trails diverge everywhere and there are people out trail-riding for the day, people out hiking, and people out plodding their token step from the car park. John Muir described them as 'overgrown frogs' who sprawled in their saddles.[9] Near to the top where the gorge's sides get closer and closer, I chose a prominent rock on which to have lunch, hoping the upward valley breeze would keep the bugs off. My bug shirt has a zip around the neck so I can open it slightly and slip the food into my mouth when the bugs aren't looking. This works only in select sites. At the top is Thousand Island Lake backdropped by Mount Ritter, Banner Peak and Mount Davis. The bugs will be bad for the next few days because this is snow-melt height—10,000 feet—and washing is difficult. I pick my spot. Put my sarong on. (Too many tourists here, you never know who might emerge around a corner.) Take boots and socks off and run into the water still wearing the bug net and top. Cover the legs in water and wash, in a contorted way without removing the bug net. Then it's leap out and slap on the repellent as fast as you can. God, these things are horrible.

You'll remember trail names: that everyone has to have one. Well people keep trying to 'name' me. First there was 'Mickey' as my thrift-shop fleece has a Mickey Mouse on it. (Tried, more out of embarrassment than the weight issue, to remove this, but couldn't.) Then there was 'British Bullock'. Not the most flattering at first sound but was intended as a compliment for the Carver uphill charge. Spitfire has also come up. Kris and I got so desperate at one stage that we chose the most bizarre and horrendous names we could think of: Armitage and Baldrick. Well the last few days I have been travelling with Hobbit. Hobbit saw me in my bug cocoon and said, "It's a butterfly about to emerge!" And hence I am now 'named' "Chrysalis".

Hobbit is an experienced hiker and a purist. He rages against those people that skipped sections like the Mojave or even the three miles around Warner Springs. He rants against those who dare to walk without a pack (slack-packing) on the odd day or two and he positively froths at the mouth on telling me that he met three hikers (the straw-hat people) who were actually walking—*can you believe it?!*—in the wrong direction—*it's just cheek!*—so they could go downhill—*downhill!*—instead of up—*that is **not** a thru-hike!*

"But how? They'd end up in the wrong place," I ask.

"They got some motel guy to drive them round and up to the top of Ralston Peak, you know just after Cajon Pass, then they walked down and then he drove them back up again the next day."

"Jammy Bastards! How cool is that!" I say in wonder.

Hobbit looks at me.

"Not that I've ever, oh no, err, just . . . well."

Hobbit salubriously invited me into his tent tonight.

"No, no, I love it out here, honest."

It would perhaps have been better inside—4 a.m. and thud thud thud woke me up, a BIG and I mean **HUGE**, shaggy bear walking past my nose, round my sleeping bag to my food bag in the tree. It tore apart the rubbish but kindly left me my toiletries—this bear at least knows that zinc oxide (for the feet) wouldn't mix with Skin So Soft. Kris almost managed to convince me that the Avon Lady product was the latest thing in bug repellent. It keeps away the odd few, but the swarms are just laughing. Deet, since purchased in Vermilion Valley, is a lot more effective if slightly toxic. I have become known in hiker circles with some awe not as the girl who walks without a stove—strange—or the girl who walks without a tent—stupid—but as the girl who came through the Sierras without any Deet . . . .

Hobbit has a bear container, so the remainders of my food were thankfully safe, although the yellow string bag is in tatters. Four women a few hundred yards from us had their food in the new bullet-proof (do bears carry guns?) anti-bear bags. The bear had them open within seconds.

So down into Yosemite where the meadows and woods of Lyell Canyon abounded with pikas, field-mice, deer and birds. A beautiful walk along a see-through silver-green river where the tourists kept popping up annoyingly. The word 'Yosemite' is a corruption of the word for Grizzly Bear in the language of the original people of the area. Grizzlies used to range all over the Sierras, but have been chased out by over-zealous hunting and the advance of suburbia. The last one was seen in California in 1924. Now if there were grizzlies still here, I might well think twice about hiking.

Day 78—935.7 trail miles north
Tuolumne Meadows

No food. No money. No box. No friends! Too many tourists. I'm lonely. Had enough. At what point could one say: "Sorry, not enjoying it any longer, going home . . . ." Probably never. Suddenly had enough of the freedom in my life.

Ok, it's not quite that bad.

I arrived at 2.10 p.m. and missed the post office by ten minutes, so I couldn't pick my box up. There is no ATM/cashpoint here and I have very little cash. Also everything in the one shop is horrendously expensive. I phoned Charles, the everybody-needs-guy (grab the opportunity, bite the bullet kind of thing).

"I'm busy."

Oh. Fine.[10]

There are three distinct groups of people here—retired tourists of all nations laden with cameras, young trendy North American climbers, and a group of lads from the British Army, definitely still with the Boy Scout method rather than the Ray Jardine one, hiking the John Muir Trail. Being surrounded by all these people after the silence of the hills and your own company suddenly makes you feel very alone. I need to take a rest day. My feet are sore and I'm generally tired. My lovely boots not so comfortable anymore. Perhaps I'll buy some insoles. It's been 12 days since I last stopped, except for half a day at Vermilion Valley, and I've done just under 200 miles over eleven passes all over 10,000 feet and climbed Mount Whitney. But to spend the day sitting in the campground with all these tourists?

There's a huge snobbery attached to travelling, and hikers are certainly not exempt. 'Travellers' look down on gap-year students who look down on back-packers who all collectively reserve their most vehement disgust for the 'tourist'. And none are worse than the tourist who goes on an arranged tour. Three weeks to 'do' China/Mexico/India for instance, spending each night in western hotels and each day being bussed from A to B and told exactly what to look at, why, and for how long. There is, one has to admit, a certain amount of sense to the whole practice when you're being shown round a historical building or archaeological site. But in the wilderness?

"And on our right, ladies and gentlemen, if you look out of the window you will see a mountain. The green stuff is grass, the white stuff is snow and the grey stuff is rock."

"Awesome!"

There are people, believe it or not, who come to Yosemite and just drive up the road and back down again, whilst gauping out of the window clinging to door handles as if they were sailing in a dingy across the Drake Passage. And yet I'm sure it's these same people who give little Johnny a bun and encourage him to stick his hand out of the window, once safely in the car park, to feed the nice cuddly little bears. It's amazing how people have come to have such a steadfast belief in tarmac.

The hiker snobbery extends, as you can see, to all of the above classes, but also has a pecking order of its own. There are thru-hikers (yes, thanks, quite clearly I'm aiming at the top), there are section-hikers (who get a lot of respect from thru-hikers as many one-time thru-hikers will most likely end up as section-hikers later on in life once family and job constraints apply), there are weekenders (if you must), there are day hikers (poor things) and there are those who stroll a wee way from the car park (please).

I guess I'm saying that I don't think there is anyone here who I want to talk to. "What a snob!" you cry, but people, mindless chat, litter and cars have all become a distant concept. I am lonely, but I cannot connect with these beings.

Gene has rather worryingly fallen behind. He is not getting enough protein and has developed some strange skin condition as a result. We left him at Vermilion tucking into two steaks with a side serving of five eggs. And that was just breakfast. Perhaps going without a stove wasn't quite such a good idea. Hobbit has disappeared off to meet his girlfriend and is taking a holiday. He has plenty of time as he is only walking California this year.

And it's trying to rain. I have a nasty feeling that the next week will be wet. May end up with pneumonia yet. The bivvy that I waited for in Lone Pine was apparently sent to the previous stop, Kennedy Meadows. Kennedy Meadows does not, according to the U.S. directory enquiries, have a telephone, even though we know it does because they won a court case to get one installed. Kris has written from Canada, but is worried about getting the bivvy back at all. Now, do I have the number of that JMT guy who said I could have his tent?

The entertainment is watching the climbers being rescued off Lembert Dome by helicopter.

Kris emailed to say she had been to see a physiotherapist and has tendonitis on her Achilles. The doctor says two months before she can hike again. So, all change, ever the determined, she is going to cycle to Canada. This is good. I don't know what would have happened if she had come back to walk. I don't know who was more worried about this, me or her. I didn't think about it—confront problems when you come to them (or bury your head in the sand)—and now I don't have to. I am looking forward to her being back. And not. I hope it gives her some sense of the fulfilment she deserves. I hope she is happier. We have planned to meet up in each town-stop. Is that being naïve? I've had the odd daydream about joyous reunions on dirt roads and laughing over veggie-burgers in towns. I think this may be wishful thinking. Still, it will be good to have her back here on the route with me. No more lonely towns with endless Americans saying "Oh my! You're walkin' to Canada, awesome!"

Camped in the 'hiker' section of a large car campground groaning with weekenders. I found a small dip in the ground just big enough for my horizontal body from where I could hide from any would-be-friendly tourists. Not quite Ray Jardine's idea of stealth camping, but not bad considering the circumstances. Satisfied with my neatly concealed little bed, I lay down to gaze at the odd star in between the pine trees before drifting off to sleep.

In the middle of the night (well, ten o'clock, which is pretty late for a hiker) a huge commotion woke me up. Bloody tourists, I thought. Drearily, I half sat up, just in time to startle the bear thundering towards me who then leapt over my sleeping bag. I lay down again. A bear just jumped over me. No. Did I dream that? A minute later there were a few more shouts from the same direction. I sat up again—this time extremely promptly—and caught the ranger's leading foot with my elbow, sending him sprawling into the pine needles on the other side of my sleeping bag. Whoops.

A powerful torch swung into my face as he righted himself.

"What are you doing there?!"

"Just sleeping," I replied, "promise."

He did not, however, wait for the answer, but carried on in pursuit of the bear.

In Yosemite they tag the bears that steal food. When a bear has arrived at what is considered dangerous behaviour—ripping cars open (apparently they prefer Hondas), bursting into tents, attacking humans—they take the bear and dump it in the wilderness, for the thru-hikers to cope with . . . .

I bought a new food bag, a black stuff-sack with no holes so the food can also survive against insects and rain. After two consecutive nights of bear attacks, to say nothing of the ranger, I am now completely paranoid. I wake up every hour to check my food is there, which is quite a performance. An arm has to come out of the bug net, pull the glasses in, then glasses on—which steam up immediately—then arm out to shine the pathetic beam of my Maglite. The bag being black, I can't see to tell if it's still there anyway. But I keep on trying. Tonight I'm sleeping on an open saddle with great views and my food will be away down round the corner—not visible from camping position. Deep breath, no bears, it will be all right.

It took a good half day to shake off the tourists, but they flaked off gradually as the trail started to climb again. Then followed three days of hot climbs and steep descents in and out of endless glaciated valleys. The respite was a stop at the 'Sierra Riviera' of Benson Lake, where I swam and sunned myself on the sandy beach.

'Another creek' says the Data Book. Cross another creek and you will have walked 1000 miles. 1000.1, to be precise. And those 'point ones' count. Another creek, but which creek? I've crossed several unmentioned creeks. Another creek, not a great marker, but there we go, 1000 miles. Must be the length of Britain, if not more. That's a long way. Should I have some kind of celebration? Eat an extra peanut? Sit still for an extra minute? Take a photograph?

I decided on the latter, got to the creek, couldn't find the path on the other side and totally forgot about it being 1000 miles. Well I'm not walking back. Photograph of me at 1000.something miles? Nah, just keep walking.

Then the next day I met up with one of the Menacing

Vegetables, known as Staggering Willy. (Couldn't quite manage to introduce myself as Chrysalis.) The Vegetables are a group of serious merry-makers. They began their hike in early April and go off-trail to every hot spring on the map. They've just had a holiday—from the trail—and are now starting up again. Staggering Willy took longer than the others and so has to catch them up. Their collective trail name comes, I am told, from a phrase in the guide book for Southern California with the mountain misery and giant asparagus;

Leaving the menacing vegetation behind, we now climb . . .

Across a creek (another creek) and suddenly, dramatically, the landscape changes. Grey granite mountains, pine trees, lakes and mosquitoes give way to red volcanic slate mountains with NO MOSQUITOES!!!!!! Free at last. Which is good as the Deet had started to add a scaly reptile quality to my legs. Gone with the mosquitoes are the lakes to wash and swim in each day. The volcanic rock is much more porous than the granite and so water drains easily away from the surface. It will however, be a brief respite, as we are soon to enter granite again, but please, please don't let the mosquitoes come back.

The volcanic side is barren and exposed. Majestic. Neon lichen colours the rocks, and wild flowers, of purples yellows reds, sprawl across the crumbly scree: molden monkey, pussy paw, matt lupin, phlox, mule's ear, sky rocket, mountain pride, mariposa tulip, penny royal, sulphur flower, horsemint, owl's clover, alpine stonecrop, blue flax, elephant snouts, shooting star. (The Menacing Vegetable, who isn't the slightest bit menacing, has a flower book with him; I'm learning.)

The slope on the other side is just as pretty but not nearly so accommodating. Large snowfields peter out into scree which tumbles steeply down to a rocky bowl and lake. This would not be a nice place to fall. Vague memories of the story in the book by the woman called Cindy (let's face it, an unlikely name for a hiker) begin to stir in my mind. Didn't she have a serious fall in the snow? Was it not this that was the end to her first PCT trip? Was it not somewhere after the Sierras? Somewhere like here? Perhaps I should wait for Staggering Willy who I left behind early this morning. But then I would have no chance of getting to the road at Sonora Pass and down into town to get to the post office today. And it's a long hitch to Bridgeport too. I keep going and set off across the snow. It is hard and icy and very steep. An ice-axe would definitely be handy. Crampons would be fantastic. Hiking poles would be useful. Something to dig in if I do slip. Gloves would be quite nice too. There's a point you arrive at, when crossing a large snow patch without equipment, usually about a third of the way across, when you look down and realise just how far it is to the bottom. And just how precarious your grip—grip? Did I say 'grip'? More like balancing act—is. And then the voice of reason:

"Don't look down. Look where you are going. And keep moving. Steadily. Slowly."

That was much more dangerous than anything in the high Sierras. A scary experience for Cindy. The area is named The Emigrant Wilderness. I pity any emigrants coming through here at any time of the year.

Day 86—1089.8 trail miles north
Echo Lake

Fantastic Foods are fantastic. Kris managed to get them to donate 14 pounds of dried humous and 14 pounds of dried taboule. Without the stove this is essential food for me. The taboule was great at first, but is now getting a little harder to eat (too much of a good thing). The humous continues to fill me up. I don't think though that I can eat much more rehydrated pasta. Let's face it, it's disgusting. A month of eating cold food. I would like an enormous plate of spinach and lentil dahl; then a baked cheesecake; then some spinach and feta cheese filo parcels; then a plate of roasted vegetables including shallots and leeks; then an apple pie with clotted cream; then a large bowl of salad with avocado; then some freshly baked white bread with unsalted butter; then some fresh strawberries; then some salmon; and a slab of mature Scottish cheddar; and potatoes, mashed potatoes, roast potatoes, new potatoes; and fresh green asparagus and raw carrots from the garden and peas, I want some peas!

Ok, enough of this torture.

Bumped into father-and-son team again (Seth and Rick from Oregon) who had flip-flopped, i.e. walked north to Tehachapi, then gone up to Oregon and started walking back in the other direction. That way they go through the Sierras with no snow difficulties and fewer mosquitoes. And with them came the stories of who's ahead and how many days and a few other bits of gossip.

Hawkeye and hiking-partner Tweedle sleep out as I do, but with bivvies to protect them from the rain. One night Hawkeye was sound asleep and snoring when Tweedle woke him up.

"Someone hit me over the head with a rock!"

"No, don't be silly, it was a bad dream," replied Hawkeye.

Then he heard the drip drip drip of blood on to the building wrap.

It was dark and they had only meagre torches, but they did what they could in bandaging the wound. By first light Tweedle had lost a litre of blood and was delusional. Hawkeye ran six miles for help and Tweedle was helicoptered out. Then Hawkeye (a very relaxed, chilled, mild-mannered guy with long grey hair and a penchant for smokeable grasses) found himself being questioned due to the suspicious nature of the wound.

"So Mr. err. 'Hawkeye', know your friend well do you?"

"Yeah, yeah man."

"Get on well with each other do you?"

"Yeah, yeah cool man."

"Ever argue at all?"

"Ahh, well you know, the odd fight over the errr, well the . . . ."

Answer? Not Hawkeye, but deer. Deer, it seems, do not recognise humans as humans when they are horizontal in fluffy sacks. As with anything they are not sure of, but inquisitive about, they lift a hoof and give it a good pawing. '*THRU-HIKER MAIMED BY DEER.*' I mean, taken out by a mountain lion . . . attacked by a bear . . . bitten by a rattlesnake . . . stung by a scorpion . . . —

there are a lot of sensational possibilities on the PCT, but deer attacks?

Pushed hard to arrive at Echo Lake Resort, to do 18 and a half miles before two o'clock, when the post office closes. Arrived and there was pitifully little, not even any hot food. I asked where I could wash my hands and was told "in the lake". All this was obviously made much worse by the fact that Staggering Willy and I had been salivating over dream-food for the last few days. In desperation I tried to reason over the notion of craving. You only crave things which it is reasonably possible to get, I told Staggering Willy. If you stop eating something for long enough then you won't crave it. He didn't look impressed and wandered off, saying he would be back later. Quite clearly he's right and it's not true. The food I crave is specific food, food from home—not pancakes or burgers or French bloody Fries (can someone please tell the Americans how to make chips?). Funny how everyone accuses British food of being bland and boring. American food? I have one word to say about that: cheese. Cheese, I mean cheese . . . . They don't actually have cheese here. They have 'Swiss cheese' which is white and vaguely stringy and doesn't even have any texture let alone taste, then there's 'Dutch cheese' which no Dutch person would remotely recognise, and lastly, the strongest 'mature' cheese you can find, 'American cheese' which is processed slices of alarmingly orange squares.

Is it all to do with the fact that cows aren't native to the country? Is that why the chocolate also tastes of nothing? More likely it is down to the legal system. Cheese is, after all, basically bacteria, and cheese that tastes is really well-grown mould. Someone somewhere must have sued the company that fed them a great slice of mature Irish cheddar or ripe French Camembert. I heard that someone did sue the Park for not warning them it could rain. When entering a National Forest it now says 'Caution: the elements can be dangerous'. Can I sue Echo Lake for not having hot food? God I need a drink!

Ezra (Staggering Willy) returned, grinning. I was still sat at the picnic table staring glumly into the lake. He plonked a bottle of Baileys and a bag of potatoes down on the table. Instant mood change. This is good. He had walked to the car park and met a local who said he would drive him a mile to the main road and then he could hitch from there the 15-odd miles to South Lake Tahoe. They got talking. Staggering Willy told him about the trail, the hike, the hikers.

"Why are you going into Tahoe?" asked the local.

"Actually," confessed Staggering Willy, "alcohol," hoping that the guy wasn't a teetotaller.

"Liquor?" said the guy, and with that gesture so typical of these hospitable Americans. "Hell, I could do with some liquor, I'll drive you there. We better cross the border into Nevada, it'll be cheaper there."

"Right," says Staggering Willy, back at the picnic table, "go and get me three empty cans," jerking his head at the overflowing recycling bin. "I'm going to make you a stove so you can cook these 'chips' you keep going on about."

Ezra made me a stove. Took three tin-cans and cut them up and now I have a stove which weighs practically nothing. A miracle. First he made holes around the rim of the bottom end of one of the cans. Then he cut out its centre bit. Then he cut the whole can in half and discarded the top bit. Then he cut a central chunk out of another of the cans and cut it down one side so it could overlap, making a cylinder. Then he cut the third can in half and again discarded the top half. The cylinder went inside the first end, which then all went inside the second end. There were some extra designer cuts to do with physics; I was very impressed by the whole process. Perhaps I should have paid more attention at that send-off party competition.

I christened it with some of Ezra's white spirit and tried to fry chips which did take a little bit longer than they take in the chippy, but hey, hot food cooked on my own stove and pure creamy alcoholic fat; I'm not complaining. By this time we had caught up with the rest of the Vegetables and so a party of hiker-sorts was in order.

You get a very different perspective of fat content and calories out here—i.e. the more the merrier. It's wonderful to have such a healthy relationship with food. Not that I've ever had a problem with eating, but however relaxed and free you are, you're always thinking to some extent, "No, I shouldn't really," or looking at the fat percentage on something stupid like yoghurt. It's not simply that I can eat without worrying (actually I need to eat more—getting thinner now, but I just can't carry it), it's that my body tells me exactly what to eat and how much. Literally it says 'fat' or 'protein' so I eat ice-cream—or in this instance Baileys—or steak, though neither have ever been a big part of my diet before. In fact before this trip I'd only ever had three steaks in my entire life and was vegetarian for ten years. Oh well.

I said a sad goodbye to Ezra and the Vegetables at Echo Lake and set off to walk through the Desolation Wilderness. They said, "Stay, stay and walk with us." Tempting. But no chance of reaching Canada. 20 miles a day. Come on girl. It's becoming easier to think about not going on, or harder to think about going on. My feet hurt too much. I doubt whether I can sustain this pace for the next three months—not without permanent injury. But more than that the will has gone. I don't wake up each morning thrilled to be here anymore. I don't feel any sense of achievement in walking more and more miles each day. My throat rejects the food it's offered. I'm in need of sustenance. I want to be at home. Perhaps it's company I'm lacking. Perhaps this place really is desolate and anyone who enters is overcome by misery and weighed down with sadness as they wander by the cold boulders and cold blue lakes. Then again perhaps not. I think I need some input. A book would be good, but to carry extra weight? No thank you.

I wish I knew where I was going. It's not Canada. 'Canada' has just become an arbitrary term for arrival at a destination. Will I really be satisfied when I get to Canada? Will I know where I'm going, what I'm doing? Will I know what I want?

All those people who came to the 'New World' blindly believing in the destination, all those people who are still coming now on increasingly hazardous trips—for them destination is all.

"When we get to America . . ."

What? To live in freedom, to work, to be able to earn money, to live without hunger, to live where there's medicine, to live without fear. Destination is all. And it can't ever be exactly what they expected. There must be huge disappointments. But still, to be able to live with hope, there's no 'hard touch' immigration policy that will overrule a desire so imperative.

It is only the privileged who go for the journey rather than the destination. We go to map, to conquer, to document. We go to photograph, to tour, to travel-write. We go for our CVs and for our rites-of-passage. We go for our indolent selves. We call ourselves adventurers, explorers. We listen in awe to those who come back and compete in pubs with our tall stories; "When I was in XXX . . . ." When other people travel we call it economic migration. Ironically their horrendous journeys stumbling through minefields, over high mountain passes in bitter weather, across countries huddled on lorries, crammed into containers on ships—it is their journeys which are the real adventures, fraught with fear and uncertainty.

The privileged go for the journey because they can come back. Canada? Canada is just a far off place where it might be pertinent to stop. It doesn't really matter where I walk as long as I walk. I'm not giving up now. I know that it's possible, but some of the challenge has gone. I've done three months, I've walked a long way, all that is good. But I'm not stopping just because it's not new any longer. I will keep going. I'm not giving in. I don't care about Canada, but I'm damn well going to walk there.

It is 15 days and 280 miles since I had a shower, 25 days and 500 plus miles since I washed my clothes in anything other than an ice-cold stream. Is this the 1000-mile blues? Come on girl. You've walked from Mexico to Lake Tahoe (the shimmering blue mass now in view). That's bloomin' miles!

Think small. Think to the next stop. A short stretch this one. Three days time and I'll be at Trail Angels Molly and Bill's House at Pooh Corner on Donner Lake. There I can buy alcohol for my new stove and start cooking hot. There will be a tent from Rich, a JMT-hiker I met at Vermilion Valley. There will be showers, washing-machines, beds, hot food, fruit juice, fruit. And also, there will be Kris.

In the afternoon the mosquitoes had gone and I met three hiking ladies in their prime (one aged 80, who completed the Appalachian Trail aged 77). Formidable. How can I be so pathetic as to complain? I'm young and healthy and this is pah, nothing! And then as if by design, the trail followed the crest-line of a cliff for the next 25 miles. I forgot my woes, took my pack off and jumped up and down turning circles in the air. I'm King of the Castle! On top of the world!

That's more like it.

Day 88—1130.1 trail miles north
Ward Peak

"Boy that was a long way up!" exclaims the day-hiker, a mile or two from the road. "Where are you coming from?"

"Oh, Mexico," I say coolly, and saunter on by.

Hah!

THREE MONTHS OF WALKING

Day 89—1150.1 trail miles north
Old Highway 40 near Donner Pass

Stopped at Bill and Molly's, a beautiful waterfront wooden house on Lake Donner; kayaking on the lake, sleeping on the comfort of cushions, hot tub and showers. Heaven. Two south-bounders, John and Hamsa were also staying. They got married overlooking Mount Shasta in Northern California and hiked off into the distance for their honeymoon. Hamsa told me that they chose the site of their wedding in winter. They went up into the mountains and found a beautiful clearing in the trees, just in front of the lake with the perfect pyramid-shaped mountain behind it. They noted down the directions for their friends and, several months later on the morning of the wedding, they drove up to find their 'spot'. The snow had all melted and only the mountain was still white. Arriving at the lake, they failed to find the clearing—what had appeared to be a snow-covered field in winter was actually part of the lake frozen over. So they had to spend the next hour frantically searching for a clearing in which to get married and then leave signs for their guests.

John is a vegan chef, an excellent chef, and we have feasted like royalty and gorged like rich Romans. Norman (a ski-patrol friend of Bill's, on hiker duty while Bill and Molly visited a new grandson) spent the day taking me shopping for insoles and finally I splashed out on a pair of customised feet. I had to stand on a machine while it gave a computer reading of my soles: high arches—left one so high that it doesn't even touch the floor. Most people walk from their heel along the outside of their foot and push off from the cushioning pad using toes to balance. I walk straight from heel to cushion and wobble a lot on the way, generally pronating (in plain English that's pigeon-toed). Anyway, now I have an insole that is moulded to the shape of my foot, giving support to my collapsing arches. Fingers, or should it be toes, crossed.

For early emigrants, there were four ways to go west. By the end of the summer I suppose I'll have crossed or passed all four of these trails, often unknowingly. There was the Oxbow route which left from Tipton, Missouri, crossed Arkansas and then plunged into the scarily named 'unorganised territory' before dipping into Texas and New Mexico and emerging somewhere near San Diego, hitting Los Angeles and cruising on up the coast to San Francisco. Then there was the 'Old Spanish Trail' which left from Independence went up over Raton Pass and crossed the Rio Grande at Santa Fe, going south through Utah Territory before heading towards Los Angeles. From Westport, Missouri, the Oregon Trail followed the Kansas River and then drifted north to run alongside the North Platte River to Fort Laramie in Nebraska Territory together with the Mormon Trail, which left from Nahvoo, Illinois. Just before Salt Lake City and Fort Bridge the trail forked north, crossing into Oregon Territory at Fort Boise, heading to Walla Walla and Portland.

The California Trail diverged from the Oregon Trail in between Bridger and Boise and crossed the Sierras via a route found by John Sutter that came in by Lake Tahoe to Lake Donner, arriving finally at the enclosure built by Sutter that would later become the capital of California, Sacramento. Following this route in the nineteenth century, a group of 100-odd people including the Donner family left a little late in the year to 'Go West' in their horse-drawn carts. They managed maybe 15 miles a day, the women working from dusk until dawn to feed and clothe the family, and always with the constant fear of attacks from Amerindians, wild animals, the unknown. They reached the Sierras late—October maybe—and found the 'road' was not even a track. They started dumping their possessions, whipping the horses, praying each night, but the weather was turning. Eventually there was nothing for it but to stop. They set up poor make-shift shelters at one end of the then unnamed Donner Lake, and settled in for the winter. The snow fell and the snow fell. They lived off mice and twigs and even resorted to eating their own shoes. They were hungry, ill-prepared and one by one they began to die. No one will ever know who took the first step—or perhaps it was even a subconscious collective decision—but when there were no more mice or shoes, and twigs could not satisfy, they moved on to their own dead. Did they kill each other to survive? That we will never know, but it was the women and children (about 40 of them) who were finally rescued in December 1846, with their husbands and fathers inside them.

It is summer here now and the views look strange—hillsides of forest with missing strips, deep grooves scarred into weird formations, chairs hanging in bizarre places. A ski-resort out of season. In the winter Tahoe and its surrounding area receive a good 8-10 feet of snow and the first falls are not so far away.

Day 91—1153.1 trail miles north
Interstate 80

Kris came and went; set off on her bicycle to find an alternate route to Canada.

Day 94—1210.2 trail miles north
County-line

A 'nothing special' two days of slack-packing (whoopee!), thanks to Molly, to Sierra City with Willy Color, a photographer hoping to make a book of the trip. At last another thru-hiker still planning to get to Canada. Perhaps I'll make it. Then up 3000 feet to the fire lookout of the volcanic Sierra Buttes. Now I'm snug as a bug in a rug, safe in the haven of a beautiful tent. A good thing too as the thunder clouds have been building up all day.

I was just about to climb into the tent this evening when I

heard the bells of a cattle herd on the move. Stayed out to watch, and then with concern as they came pouring over the hill in a direct line for the tent. The cowboys hauled the cattle off but 'Camp' (the dog) ran straight in and made himself comfortable at the end of my sleeping bag. 'Camp' is 'camped' and will not leave. I yanked him out of the tent but I can't shut the door because his nose is stuffed through the zip. Camp seems to want to stay.

A hiker ahead, I have heard, has been adopted by a dog. A beautiful wolfhound began shadowing him one day and now is firmly attached. The crunch came when the hiker was hitching into town; the dog leapt into the truck after him. The dog has decided to walk to Canada. Luckily for me (I am NOT carrying Pedigree Chum the rest of the way) the cowboys returned to take Camp home.

Several ranches retain rights to graze their cattle in designated 'wilderness' areas. (A 'wilderness' = no roads, no motorised vehicles, no permanent settlements and limited hunting and fishing activities.) In the Sierras it is a tradition that has been going for '*several generations*', says the guide book, to bring the cattle up for the summer grass and then take them down to the valley to winter. Several generations easily makes a tradition in the States. I have heard complaints from other hikers who advocate a cattle-free wilderness. The ranch owners would probably argue that hikers do as much damage as their cattle anyway.

Do we damage the wilderness trekking along our paths through the trees? It seems most American hikers adhere to 'leave no trace' principles, i.e. they carry out what they carried in. There is at least a notable lack of toilet paper, unlike other famous and popular hiking trails such as Annapurna, Nepal, or the Inca Trail, Peru. The hikers here complain about the horses and the pack trains—a row of mules carrying equipment for tourists, or supplies to rangers—claiming that they spoil the trail and its surroundings with their dirt and capacity for churning the ground to pulp. Horses were only introduced to the area in 1775. It is true that in some places one has to struggle through shin-deep sand due to horse activity but really it's nothing to complain of when I think of the deep wet clay mud baths I've walked through in Britain.

So Kris. Time has not resolved the issues surrounding Kris's departure. She is hurt and angry. She has written me a ten-page letter to which I am to reply. Yes I could have been more sympathetic. Yes I could have put friendship before my own goal. Shackleton put his men first and gave up the polar expedition, and lost not one life. Scott's ambition ending up killing them all. One was a great leader, and the other was not.

This is not however, a polar expedition.

She's angry with me for not believing that she had a serious injury. But then tendonitis does not happen in one day. I know I did what I was meant to do (we stopped, we rested, we waited), but she is angry because I did not want to do it. Angry because I did not believe in her, because I thought that she didn't want to be there. I know what she says is true, but I cannot explain to her this overwhelming desire to walk. I've tried saying sorry but she's still angry.

I realise now why all the groups of three guys had their own tents. If you want to do something like this your goals have to be identical, your commitment equal. And you have to be able to do the same number of miles a day as each other. Otherwise one will get frustrated and the other will get resentful. And even if you have the same ambition it's better I think to go alone, meet people as you walk, be independent. Perhaps I'm just not a good team player. Or perhaps living with someone 24 hours a day through sweat and smell and heat is not conducive to teamwork.

I want to walk as far as I can. I don't know anymore how important reaching Canada is. And I know my feet might very well stop me from getting there. But I want, given the right weather, to walk as far and as well as I can. And I don't want to be stopped.

Since I've been on my own, my 'regime' has been different. Wake up with the birds at around half past five, leave by 6.30. Walk two hours, break; walk two hours, break; walk two hours, lunch at 1 p.m. for two hours. Then meander along in the afternoon usually until about six-ish. Average: 20 miles a day. Today I left at seven o'clock and did 15 and a half miles by one o'clock. Thing is: what to do with all the spare time? I swim whenever possible. Can't walk more miles, even though there are plenty of hours left, as feet and body start saying stop around 20 miles however fast I've walked them.

Right now I'm perched on the corner of a rocky switchback; 21 and a half miles, no camping place in sight for another three or four miles. Safe in my tent I can watch the bugs trying to get inside. If it's not ants, it's mosquitoes, if not mosquitoes, flies, if not flies, midges—tonight all of them. Without the tent I'd have to be inside my sleeping bag (rated to minus seven degrees) with fleece on and head and arms inside the bug net. Stewing. As it is I'm sweating in just a sarong. Thank you (Angel!) for sending me this beautiful beautiful tent.

I've given up on a water filter. (Picked up a tent and a stove, disposed of the water filter.) And now I wish I'd done this a lot sooner. They say it isn't healthy to consume iodine for six months, but you really don't have to. Southern California for all its water scarcity, boasts several beautiful springs which one could, in hindsight, drink from without any worry. In the Sierras it isn't difficult to find water just coming off a snowmelt or up from underground and as long you're careful not to take water from below where cattle may have been you're normally all right. And on the odd occasion you have a bit of diarrhoea, well it's not going to kill you, probably make you stronger in the long run. America on the whole is exceptionally clean—glinting, sparkling advert clean. The other hikers are paranoid about the water-born bacteria, giardia. It is a risk, but the water filter weighed too much, kept breaking and definitely wasn't worth it.

Coming down round the uninspiringly named Gibralter Mountain (resemblance isn't overwhelmingly apparent), I arrived upon two women in their 50s in bras and shorts, hacking away at a log with a pick-axe. They are attempting to ride part of the trail (they had taken their horses back up the mountain the night before on discovering this tree) and came prepared with tools. The pickaxe, however, was about one twelfth of the width of the fallen tree. I helped for a bit, then carried on down trail to discover the next four to five miles strewn with trees. I scrambled round them, clambered over them and even had to take off my pack and wiggle my way underneath a huge trunk on one occasion. The sides of the valley are too steep and overgrown to go round. Sorry, not going five miles back uphill to tell you, but good luck girls!

At the bottom I could hear the roar and whine of chain-saws and people: a trail crew. There were three people eating their lunch beside a stream. I greeted them and told them about the plight of the two ladies up the hill, and asked if they could go and help them cut down the fallen trees. They nodded but then, as I carried on around the corner, one muttered, "I'm not going all the way back up there again."

Oh no, poor ladies, I thought. And the trail crew did have a motorbike with them, so it wouldn't really have been that difficult.

The PCT is banned to all vehicles—only humans, horses and pack-trains are allowed. In wilderness areas the rangers/trail crew are not even allowed to use any motorised equipment and have to clear the trees with two-man saws. One hiker told me once that he was walking along when he heard a motorbike coming. He planted himself in the middle of the trail and made the man stop.

"Do you realise you're on the Pacific Crest Trail?" he confronted the stranger.

The guy assented.

"Do you realise that you cannot ride a motorbike down this trail?" and then, just in case he was being a little too aggressive, "There are rangers around you know, you can be fined."

"I am the ranger," said the guy.

"Oh."

When you are the law, I guess you can break it.

I carried on and met more and more small groups of trail crew. I told each and everyone of them about the two women up on the hill in the hope that one would be the leader of the group and make sure someone went back up. Who knows what happened?

All the way down to the Feather River (2900 feet) and then all the way back up the other side through forests of black oak, sycamore, alder, pine and dogwood and a trail full of poison oak and black fly. I've decided that since the views aren't, well, tremendous, I'm going to be a wild flower photographer instead. Gone mad on recording every single wild flower.

Field of wild flowers

LONELINESS

Day 98—1283.2 trail miles north
Belden

I used to be scared of losing food. Now I'm just scared. I know that most bears run on seeing a human. And besides they are, or are meant to be, diurnal. It's the ones that come in the night that are after your food. Seems silly when so many hikers sleep with their food beside them, inside the tent—why would a bear attack me when my food is hung on a tree away from me? Even ended up singing in the middle of the night: "Oh Lord, I've travelled so hard . . . ."

Stop being scared; it's not logical.

As you approach a road each time the number of people dramatically increases. After three or four days of your own company, the first people you meet are greeted like long lost friends and you explain everything about your trip, forgetting that they've just come up from showers and civilisation and you look (and smell) like a dishevelled rat. Then the next group ten minutes further on get a little less information, and then less and less until the final day-trippers right beside the road are lucky to get even a nod. The way down to Belden was steep however, switchback after switchback, and no-one was going up. As I approached the valley I could hear the road and railway and practically ran down in my excitement. People, food, showers! Belden turned out not to be what one could call a town. It was a group of wooden huts that looked like an army outpost from the colonial era.

Kris had left my box behind the desk with the woman in the store, who had ever-so-kindly decided to put it outside with the Hiker Box. The Hiker Box is a communal dumping ground for unwanted food. It's like an exchange—you can't eat any more of your food, so you throw in whatever you have and take out whatever you fancy. So there was all my food up for grabs and sure enough all the good food (Mars bars, hot chocolate) had gone, and there was a paltry supply of rice and pumpkin seeds left. Luckily my contact lenses were still floating around—they really are the most important thing and something I couldn't be happy without— and also another ten-page letter of grievances left by Kris which must have made good reading for all and sundry. I smiled sourly at the woman behind the desk and bought chocolate bars to replace mine from her extortionately priced stock while she smiled slightly smugly back at me. There was a handful of people but no-one to talk to; I felt homesick for the trail. How will I be able to function in society after this? All I want is the peace of walking and to be out of this 'town' as soon as possible. The shower was only slightly less grotty than me. What I do miss is being clean, really clean; being able to wash each day with soap and hot water. The dirt and dust are fine, but the sweat and grime are not.

The shower room has a big cracked dirty mirror, and I realise that mirrors are not something I miss particularly. It has been lovely not to have to look at myself and consider my appearance for the outside world. I do actually have a mirror with me. A very small one; I use it to put my contact lenses in each morning so it's not a luxury or an unnecessary weight. It's a small piece of mirror to be more exact, that Kris found in Bolivia and I used it when hiking then, for the same purpose.

What I mean is there are no shop windows in which to glance to check out your shape as you walk by. There are no glossy magazines everywhere or posters with women who have had every fold, orange-peel and stretch-mark airbrushed off them. There are no stick-thin thirty-five-year-old 'girls' in stick-thin clothes still trying to look like they're fifteen. There are no images. I am free from society saying what I should look like, what I should wear, what I should do. I wear practical things; shorts that are many sizes too big, for comfort and ease of walking. At night I wear a thermal top that cannot be said to be attractive by any stretch of the imagination. And when I meet people on the trail or coming into town, I don't think of my spots or my bum or my hairy legs and armpits or greasy hair. I think of the fact that I've walked however many miles it is. I feel proud to be me. I feel strong. Free.

Perhaps it's just me. What am I trying to say? That I feel more hiker than 'woman', that the other hikers I meet I see as more hiker than 'man'.

After Belden on the Middle Fork Feather River (2300 feet) the trail has been washed away, so we're on a diversion. Like all diversions, it's extremely well sign-posted at the beginning (i.e. '*Follow these bright orange arrows*') and then not. I've walked seven miles on a steep grade (up to 6753 feet) and I've only seen one arrow, the first one with the diversion sign. Ah well, at least I'm still on the map.

Hamsa and John, the couple I met going southbound at Donner Lake, had forewarned me about this part. They reached a notice at the northern end, saw an orange arrow and followed it. They walked for about thirteen miles following orange arrows and ended up exactly where they had left the trail, by the sign explaining about the landslide and diversion. (They found out later there had been a biking rally there the day before and the arrows were not intended for hikers.) Frustrated, they camped the night and set off the next day, thinking they would try the trail—how bad could it be?

Nine miles or so in they reached the wash-out. The cliff had collapsed and blocked the valley. It took them a while but they scrambled over the boulders; lowered, threw and passed up their packs from one to the other, and crossed the landslide. Feeling victorious they had a break and then walked on, only four miles or so to Belden; they could sleep in town tonight. Half a mile on they came across another landslide. This one was even bigger, more difficult, very time consuming but they made it over, only scratched legs the worse. Then came the third wash out. There was no way round, no way over, no way through and at the end of the day they had to admit defeat, only three miles from Belden. The next day they walked and climbed and struggled all the way back to the sign saying 'Diversion' where Hamsa sat down in despair. Luckily a local rancher turned up in his jeep and set them off in the right direction (the one without the orange arrows).

For me, it was fine. Going northbound is much easier than going southbound—PCT posts/signs are designed and placed to be easily noticeable to the northbound hiker and hidden to anyone coming in the opposite direction.

Day 99—1310.1 trail miles north
Humboldt Summit

A fairly lazy day. Arrived at Humboldt Summit, where the Humboldt road reaches the pass over the mountains. There seem to be a lot of Humboldts in North America, but Humboldt County, California, at least, was named in 1850 after the naturalist Alexander von Humboldt. The guide book warned not to camp there as it could be a hangout for *'gun-crazed drunks'*, rather than naturalists, but there was only one other human there, an artist called Robin Brierley on the slow road to Canada (slightly faster than me—by car), selling cards along the way. Born in Zimbabwe, he left home at the age of 14 to go and live with an illegal prospector, killing and roasting turtledoves on a spit to get by. He suggested that I caught grouse to increase my protein intake. There are certainly enough of them—big fat chicken-sized grouse, with ruff-skirts. A whole tribe of chicks will wait until the last minute before making their presence known and then scare the living daylights out of you and themselves as they squawk and flap in all directions. Sometimes the mother 'dies' in front of you, trailing a broken wing along the path or just plummeting dead out of the sky, in order to draw you away from her nest and chicks. They have got 'dying' down to a fine art—more melodramatic than a Brazilian soap-opera.

So I hung out with Robin for a few hours admiring the view of Lassen Peak (10,407 feet), a huge *'dome of pasty lava'*—guide book—that soars up above the other rolling hills around it. Nice to have some company. And he fed me oranges and bananas and cod-liver oil. Lassen Volcanic National Park (named after a Danish immigrant who pioneered the first route for the settlers into Northern California) is a hotchpotch of steaming cracks of red earth, sulphurous lakes and pine trees which grow rather incongruously beside murky water too hot to touch. It is home to some of North America's most famous hot springs, though most, unfortunately, lie too far off-trail to visit.

I have taken to singing songs as I walk along, this time not just to keep my feet moving evenly, but to occupy my mind. For the first time I understand why folk songs have quite so many verses to them—when walking there are never enough. I sing *Cockles and Mussels Alive Alive O* and *She'll be Coming Round the Mountain When She Comes* and *Oh My Darling Clementine*. I must be the only person in the world who knows all the words to *What Shall We Do With the Drunken Sailor?* And when I have sung them all several times a day, I write and ask my friends to send me more. I walk along muttering *The Lady of Shallot*, attempting to exercise my brain simply by learning lines. Someone sent *Didn't it rain!* and I sang it as I trotted along the trail in the heat. That night there was a huge thunderstorm and the skies opened: didn't it rain! I am so grateful for this tent. And so lucky to have made it through the Sierras without one.

The sun, an orange ball, is setting behind the hills, lighting my tent and the volcanic rock around me in a pleasant glow. Bedtime. Sleep—and try not to wake up. I slept through an entire night at Bill and Molly's. The first time in three months. That was following my performance on the night of my arrival, when I thought another hiker going to the bathroom in the early hours was a bear. Bear = make noise. Shrieked loud enough to wake the household.

Day 100—1332.9 trail miles north
Stover Camp

Pace pace pace. 16 miles in six hours, 23-mile day. Making up for the slack one before. Easy terrain. Up to three miles an hour this morning. Pace pace pace. Lassen is beautiful.

Norman from the Donner Lake stop had told me that a place called Drakesbad Guest Ranch was a great stop, but no one had mentioned it in the hiker circle. I decided to go, then decided not to, then decided to, then not. The pros were: 1) FOOD—just not got enough with me, want to eat more and more; lost seven pounds since Agua Dulce, which isn't a worry, but bones keep jerking out; and there might be food that I might like. 2) The possibility of a shower? 3) The possibility of a phone?? 4) The possibility of a dip in the hot spring swimming pool??? All pretty good. But as I got nearer and nearer I convinced myself that as a 'Lodge' they would look me up and down and decline me any kind of service. Or if they let me eat, it would cost a small fortune. So I opted for rehydrated noodles by the side of the pale green Boiling Springs Lake, with the mud bubbling around me and the steam pouring up into the air through the red rocks. Then I carried on and there was the turning and I dwindled some more at the sight of the pool, but no. Onwards to the creek round the corner named enticingly 'Hot Springs Creek' which was anything but hot and enticing, where I washed and dried just in time before a contingent of walkers came by. The guide book says that you have to reserve years in advance to stay at the lodge, weeks in advance for a meal, and only guests could use the pool. It was pointless. But FOOD.

I went. And Andy the Chef said,

"What would you like, then?"

Got a bowl of fresh fruit salad and a package to take away: a sandwich, two dark red plums the size of apples, a nectarine, a juicy peach, delicious blackberries and an apple. Um, a little heavy, but free! So it was definitely worth the visit even if one of the staff gave me incorrect directions to get back on the trail and I walked for over a mile in the wrong direction (grrr).

Many of the Amerindian peoples had very little concept of ownership, especially when it came to food. Food was shared out equally to feed all no matter who had done the hunting or gathering. In 1862—while Lincoln was preparing to fight a civil war in the name of freedom—the Santee people were starving. They had surrendered nine tenths of their land and with it their game and access to food. In return they were promised annual payments. That year the payment was delayed but the agent refused to give them food until they had their money from the government. With a callousness that even surpasses Marie Antoinette, one of the traders said, "Let them eat grass." Not to share food when you had it was inexplicable to the Amerindian culture—unthinkably cruel. What resulted was 'Little Crow's (Ta-oya-te-duta) War' of the great plains. Perhaps this is one thing left in legacy to the modern American; their hospitality and willingness to share food, at least in rural parts.

My next treat was Doritos dipped in peanut butter. Not an everyday delight. You see, I met some Jehovah's Witnesses, who said, "We're cooking chicken, you must have some."

Ever eager for a free meal, I consented, nodding away to "Paradise will come, the Lord will send a flood to wipe the evil off the earth, and the weirdos, there's too many out there, be careful, as it says in Isaiah, Chapter Five, Verse Three . . . ." So I bought some Doritos to take along to the happy party, only to find that I was served outside, separately, alone. (This was after I'd had a shower . . . .) So full of chicken, potatoes and veg, I still had a large bag of Doritos to take away. Doritos crunched up with taboule and flaxseeds—now that was an improvement.

No water for 30 miles. So I filled up everything—six and a half litres and then my three-litre bag began to leak. No duct tape, I'd run out. Found a fire-fighter who also had no tape but gave me a litre of water. So, amidst the scores of bear footprints, I climbed up to the Hat Creek Rim with water pouring down the back of my legs from the leaking bag. Lassen at one end and then a long long valley with volcanic cinder cones leading to Mount Shasta at the other end. A day of walking along the Rim through the 1998 burn. No shade and temperatures up to 100 degrees. Fires start easily in this region. Often from sparks from machinery or trains. Often too by people. One PCT hiker is to blame for a 5,000 acre fire, started when he tried to burn his toilet paper. Much of the trail is under fire restriction (i.e. no campfires) as the risk is too high, but back with Christopher in Southern California, we had a fire one night in a campground. The wind picked up and the sparks flew—pine cones and needles burn in a flash. The burn I'm walking through now started from lightning.

Forest fires aren't, as previously thought, all bad. Many plants and trees thrive on fire—like the ceanothus shrubs of the chaparral or knobcone pines which only release their seeds after a fire. The problem is that we have prevented fires for so long that when they do happen now they are all-consuming raging furnaces that sweep over huge areas and completely destroy everything (crown fires). The fires of the indigenous people (ground fires) used to be smaller, more frequent events that burnt off the debris, provided food for deer over the re-growth period, and ultimately healthier forests.

Then the thunderclouds started gathering. My first thought was, "This is ridiculous, carrying this much water and now it's going to rain." Then, "Oh no, I might get struck by lightning!" A little melodramatic maybe, but when you're walking through the knee-high debris of a 25,000-acre forest fire started by lightning and the thunder is rolling in behind you . . . .

It blew over.

This is the hardest thing I've ever done. Only just realising this now. People said, "This will be a life-changing experience." I'm not sure I really believed them. Perhaps with someone else, if Kris had still been here, it wouldn't have been. On my own it's huge, daunting. And there are way too many hours in the day to think about nothing at all. Man is a sociable animal.

NORTHERN CALIFORNIA AND OREGON

SLACKING

Day 104—1417.5 trail miles north
Burney Falls

I'm bored. Can one be bored? Am I allowed to be bored? I've run out of fantasies. How can you run out of those? Run out of daydreams. I've been through it all: rescued children, run from danger, survived disasters and escaped oppressive regimes. I've fallen in love, had a honeymoon in Italy and lived content to a ripe old age. I've gone it alone, backpacked my toddler around developing countries, led an adventure-filled life. I've written books, given talks, and become a world-class photographer. I've written a screen-play, directed the action, filmed the cinematography and starred in the leading role. I've even managed to make Kris forgive me. That one's definitely a fantasy.

How can one run out of these things? Does that mean I've a limited imagination? Maybe I'm all thought out.

Keeping my mileage up at 23-24 miles a day, I finally managed to catch up with some other thru-hikers—Blisterfree, Sparrow Hawk, Woody and Terry—only to find they have all decided to stop in Ashland, Oregon.

"It's too late," they say. "Won't make it anyway, so I'll leave this section for another year."

Too late? Everyone I know seems to have given up: Purple and Oasis, Mudflap from Anza, Kirk the physiotherapist, John the Irishman, Christopher from the Sierras; Willie Color, on the morning I saw him last saying "see you on the trail" from Sierra City; fathers from father-and-son teams; three-boy groups dwindled to one; all six of The Family (two parents, four kids) reduced to one, Rosie, who finally stopped in Tuolumne; Bald Eagle and Nocona from Independence with altitude problems; Mike the

American air-lifted off Whitney with a broken leg; UK Ray from Echo Lake with a hernia; Aussie air-lifted off the Sierras with vertigo; Tweedle air-lifted off in Yosemite after the deer incident. Out of almost three hundred who started there are maybe seventy left.

Turtle? Are you still out there somewhere? Probably weeks ahead by now. Straw-hat girls and boy? Probably finished . . . . Could there be anyone behind me? Gene, are you still coming?[11]

Too late, too late.

Day 112—1580 trail miles north
Carter Meadows

Parents—out visiting for two weeks—so slack-packing and food. I am on holiday. Meeting up with them was not as difficult as it seemed initially. After hiking this far, I know very well how far I can hike each day and how long it will take me. So "I'll see you at 6.30 p.m. in five days time" is perfectly possible, assuming nothing goes wrong. They are here with an RV (Recreational Vehicle—the American version of a car and caravan in one unit) and each night we pour over the map, planning where we can meet the next day. This bit is much more difficult. Luckily for me, this section is not a wilderness section, so there are some roads. However, a 'road' in America does not necessarily mean a road that a mobile home can drive down. Main roads are few and far between, and the one road that the trail might cross in a day, is more often than not a jeep road, sometimes very well maintained, other times more like an old wagon trail. The first day we arranged to meet at one of these roads. On the map it looked reasonably good. I arrived and waited, and waited, and waited, watching a pair of bald-eagles circle above.

When you are on the trail it is difficult to get lost. There are very few places where there is not trail tread as such—the odd mile or two in Southern California where the off-roaders have obliterated it or where it may be obscured by snow in the mountains. Even in these places it is not easy to get lost because there are markers, or you can see the pass you are heading for. I got lost once coming up though

Kennedy Canyon before Sonora Pass. There had been a blow-down and a good chunk of trees lay blocking the path. I started walking round the trees but failed to locate the trail on the other side. No matter I thought, I can see where I'm going, and so headed straight up the slope. I was looking for a 'road' that cut into the mountain, easily visible on a treeless scree slope and sure enough there was one up ahead to the northwest. I climbed up some more and then came into view another 'road' switch-backing up to a pass to the west. Hmmm. No question of walking all the way back down again and I headed for the first option (when in doubt, go north). To my relief when I hit the road there was a PCT post just a little way down. PCT posts are square wooden posts that are about waist high. Unlikely as it may sound they do become very distinctive.

The hiker is much more likely to get lost by taking the wrong path. Other trails cross and join the PCT and are frequently unmarked. The guide book does tell of one such trail which has a signpost saying '*THIS IS NOT THE PCT*'. After a week on the trail you have a 'nose' for the look and shape of it and I'd given my parents a quick lesson in recognising the trail in the morning. On main roads there are big signposts which say '*Pacific Crest National Scenic Trail*' and one time we even had a signpost with two little walkers saying:

HIKER XING

(Xing is the American shorthand for Crossing—hence Deer Xing or Children Xing and all sorts of other stranger things including Duck Xing and even Toad Xing.) On reaching an Interstate the trail goes underneath, following the drainage built for a creek which makes for a spooky, slanted and smelly crossing. Dirt roads, however, have no such helpful signs and often the trail will reach them, walk along them for a bit and then leave them the other side. As a hiker you get very used to studying the ground. You usually know the footprints of the person in front of you, and even if you never get to meet the person you follow their tracks in good faith. Otherwise previous hikers often leave arrows drawn in the dust or even little pine cone faces.

No parents. It was about seven o'clock and getting dark. I had almost nothing with me—shorts and a sun top and a little water left over. This was not good. I set off down the road in the direction they were meant to be coming from, slightly concerned that they may have been past already. I had visions of punctures and me left alone, miles (about 12) from the nearest big road. Then I came to a road junction, one that was not on the map. Hmmm. Arranging to meet people in an area that has been logged is not something one can do by map reading. And sure enough two people had walked up it not long ago. Wishing I had made sure to know the soles of their shoes I followed the tracks and eventually found the owners staring up into the sky watching the bald-eagles—all's well that ends well, but tomorrow I'm carrying a bit more with me, even if it doesn't quite mean slack-packing.

Carrying less does mean doing more miles: 30 miles, 26, 26, and then 31 miles—covering ground speedily and getting fed wet (as in, not dried) food and fresh fruit in the mobile home each night.

This mileage sounds pretty impressive—well, I'm impressed at any rate. There are hikers however, who average over 30 miles a day with packs. The Yo-yos for instance, now reduced to one Scott Williamson, attempting for the third time to go from Mexico to Canada and back again in the same year. Word is that he has already turned around, doing at least 35 miles a day with no rest days, completing his fifth thru-hike of the PCT. Just think how many 'selves' you could find doing that.

Or the Amazons, yet to know that they have been christened the Amazons, a.k.a. the straw-hatted trio we met in Agua Dulce—two long-legged girls and a guy from South Carolina, who did a mere 40-miler from Donner Pass to Sierra City. They started a good three weeks after anyone else, took ten days holiday before the Sierras, regularly take extra days off, and are now ahead of most of the 'pack'. They climbed Mount Whitney on the same day as me, and not content with scaling the near 15,000-foot mountain and hiking a 20-mile day, Itchy and Scratchy (the girls' real trail names, after a bad case of poison oak) decided to do half an hour's sit-ups. Got to keep that upper body in shape . . . . I shall, however, follow John Muir's bidding at this point:

> *Nothing can be done well at a speed of 40 miles a day. The multitude of mixed, novel impressions rapidly piled on one another make only a dreamy, bewildering, swirling blur, most of which is unrememberable.*[12]

My father and I leave early in the morning. He walks a few miles with me and then walks back again. Each afternoon they both hike in to meet me and then we all walk back to the RV.

Two ladies and a llama: section-hiking. And the llama, in attempting to get over a large fallen ponderosa pine tree trunk, has slid down the bank and has been sitting in tree debris for two hours, face down on a steep slope; stuck.

"He's terribly sure-footed, come on Dancing Cloud, do stand up," says the one with ribbons dangling from her dark hair.

("It's because she drinks goat's milk that she doesn't go grey," whispers the other, "straight from the goat!")

But Dancing Cloud is heavily and ungainly plonked 20 yards below the narrow trail path. So my father and I, and the two llama ladies, got to work building up a bank below the llama whilst my mother took photographs. Then we all heaved him sideways to which he protested loudly. Then we heaved and we heaved but DC was definitely not going anywhere.

"He won't move his front legs," I say, between the llama groans. "Maybe he's hurt."

And then it dawns on us all that llamas stand up back legs first like camels rather than like horses. So we turn round and tug at the back end and sure enough DC rises up clumsily and then stomps back up the slope with us, rescued. The damsels in distress were full of gratitude; Dancing Cloud, however, was not so impressed and spat angrily, catching Mum in the face.

Long, long ago, when the world was so new that even the stars were dark, it was very, very flat. Chareya, Old Man Above, could not see through the dark to the new, flat earth. Neither could he step down to it because it was so far below him. With a large stone he bored a hole in the sky. Then through the hole he pushed down masses of ice and snow, until a great pyramid rose from the plain. Old Man Above climbed down through the hole he had made in the sky, stepping from cloud to cloud, until he could put his foot on top of the mass of ice and snow. Then with one long step he reached the earth. The sun shone through the hole in the sky and began to melt the ice and snow. It made holes in the ice and snow. When it was soft, Chareya bored with his finger into the earth, here and there, and planted the first trees. Streams from the melting snow watered the new trees and made them grow. Then he gathered the leaves which fell from the trees and blew upon them. They became birds. He took a stick and broke it into pieces. Out of the small end he made fishes and placed them in the mountain streams. Of the middle of the stick, he made all the animals except the grizzly bear. From the big end of the stick came the grizzly bear, who was made master of all. Grizzly was large and strong and cunning. When the earth was new he walked upon two feet and carried a large club. So strong was Grizzly that Old Man Above feared the creature he had made. Therefore, so that he might be safe, Chareya hollowed out the pyramid of ice and snow as a tepee. There he lived for

thousands of snows. The Indians knew he lived there because
they could see the smoke curling from the smoke hole of his tepee.
When the pale-face came, Old Man Above went away. There is
no longer any smoke from the smoke hole. White men call the
tepee Mount Shasta.

Shastika (California)[13]

Lots of lumbering through logging areas, then one day you suddenly come round a corner and there is Mount Shasta. Right there, looming up in front, not a distant northwards guide any longer, covered in glaciers. Here at Castella I met up briefly with the Vegetables again (they had skipped a section and hitched up here) in fine vegetable form and also a thru-hiking southbounder who had started at the Canadian border way back in June, road-walking much of Washington as the trail was snowbound. Then came Castle Crags, Gumboot Lake, Black Butte (with a *you* sound though it was shaped a bit like a butt) and endless views of Mount Shasta as we wound around it. Wandering along into the rocky Klamath Mountains (up up up) there was suddenly an astonishingly green swathe of colour. A spring and with that spring a dense mass of wild flowers: cut-leaf cone flower [*rudbecia*], sticky tofieldia [*tofieldia glutinosa*], mountain pasque flower [*anemone occidentalis*] otherwise known as 'mop flowers' (by me, as they look like miniature mops), and some Californian pitcher plants or cobra lily [*darlingtonia californica*], which look like alien wildlife. These last type consume flies and insects in their cobra-style heads.

This part of the trail was rather neglected and vegetation sprawled everywhere—sometimes so dense and strong that you literally had to fight your way through the undergrowth, barely able to see the trail tread at all. The nice bit is finding the wild gooseberries (though they're a bit sour), thimbleberries (great), Oregon grapes (none too tasty) or blueberries. The huckleberries are mostly over, but if I walk fast enough Oregon should still be laden. The nasty bit is in the lower regions where the path is swamped by poison oak. Luckily for me, I now know that I react minimally to the shiny green un-oak-like plant. Filling a bottle from a trickling spring once, I accidentally held my leg against a root of poison oak for about ten minutes. The poison comes from all parts of the plant. Apparently Amerindians were immune to it. The result for me, was a red lump which faded over time and thankfully didn't itch. The previously mentioned Itchy and Scratchy walked along the same trail as everyone else but ended up covered in an incessant rash that spread all over their bodies and gave them no rest. In desperation the girls set off for the hospital where they were greeted with a sign on the door that read:

Do NOT enter if you have a rash. Do NOT touch anything.

Waving wildly outside the glass doors they eventually managed to get the attention of a nurse who gave them antihistamines.

The guide book also warns of tick problems. Ticks cannot fly and transfer themselves to you by hanging on to the end of a piece of grass and moving over as your leg brushes against it. Walking through tick country is a good time not to have hairy legs as it is easier for a tick to latch on to hairs, or the fur of an animal. Back in Southern California, Kris found the odd one or two, but before they had done any damage. There are three big problems connected with ticks: Lyme Disease, Spotted Fever and Tick Paralysis. Luckily they are all very rare. The main problem is the nuisance factor of how to remove a tick once it has bitten you—they like to get closer than is generally desirable and bury their heads into your skin, usually in a warm part of the body, like the groin or armpits. You risk danger of infection if you decapitate the tick in your anxiety to get rid of it, leaving its head inside. Very nice. So every night after walking through grassy areas, you have to check for ticks. Which could be an interesting chat-up line should you meet the hiker of your dreams. As it is I find myself attempting to feel all over my body for any unknown small humps. I am covered in mosquito bite scars which all manifest themselves as small humps, just to make things more confusing.

Now the three of us are on the trail together, complete with tents and enough food for four days. Dad and I have hung the food bags out of bear-reach, and we are sitting round a campfire by Fisher Lake with the rough-skinned newts and bats gobbling up the mosquitoes.

We took a detour to Shadow Lake and had a refreshing swim while the helicopters, out looking for a missing 70-year-old who had left her group camp and gone for a walk alone at night, zoomed in and out of the valleys. Here is Marble Mountain Wilderness— the Marble Mountain is itself a spectacular sight and Mount Shasta is still poking up in the distance. Dad has given himself the trail name of 'Water-Carrier' as we send him off each time to find water. Mum is waiting for bears, half-hoping to see one, yet wanting to eat tomorrow. On the horizon a thick layer of forest fire smoke sits, a constant companion as America burns for the summer. Behind us the trail through Kennedy Meadows has gone up in flames and also 30,000 acres along the re-route after Belden, causing problems for south-bounders. Ahead, the trail through Oregon is as yet unaffected.

COMPANY

Day 117—1650.5 trail miles north
Seiad Valley

Came down to Seiad Valley (1371 feet) to find another three hikers. Two Jesus Freaks (their chosen trail name) and a guy called Vive, who I have a hazy memory of meeting on that first strange day at the kick-off party at Lake Morena Campground near the Mexican border. The Jesus Freaks were walking on 'Lurve and Prearr!' and, as far as I could tell, nothing else. One found a pair of shoes in the Hiker Box which were exactly his size and as his present pair had very little left to them, this was a God-send. (Literally.) They survived on Hiker Box food and berries and the kindness of the people they met. Jesus Freak One, a high-school failure from a poor neighbourhood who terrorised his fellow pupils and teachers, found God whilst on remand. He went back to school, gave a speech on the erring of his ways, and persuaded his most abused victim to go walking with him: Jesus Freak Two. They told me they were planning to do the last 60 miles in one go. That's without stopping, to walk through the day and night and day and get to the border. With little to carry, they set off that evening at a healthy lick and that was the last I heard of them. Vive, on the other hand, was keen to go a bit slower as he had been resting for a few days after an injury, and wanted to hike out with me the next day. A last frantic packing session ensued which ended with me swapping all of my clothes, backpack and sleeping bag with Mum (her things were all more expensive and therefore lighter), and then goodbye.

Vive and I walked out of the heat and dust and crossed the Californian/Oregon border the next day. The border crossing was a wooden plaque at the side of the trail half way up a switchback.

No more, no less. *'Welcome to Oregon'* on one side, *'Welcome to California'* on the other. We took the customary snaps and shared a miniature brandy.

One thousand seven hundred and six miles. Mexico to here, 1706 miles walked. And only 962 to go. Come on girl! Let's go! 900-odd miles. You can do it. At 20 miles a day, that's 40 days. 40 days to go. I can do that. And if I average just over 20, 22 say or even 23 miles, that's even less. 40 days. Today is 27th August. 40 days from now will be the first week of October. That's good. That's fine. That's ok. I'll make it before winter.

Day 123—1765.5 trail miles north
South Branch Mountain Shelter

Now hikers are usually pretty comfortable with one another. There is a large gender imbalance—as far as I know there have only been five other women travelling without male counterparts this year. The men decided that Kris and I must be gay for some unknown reason and this rumour kept us 'safe' from some of the inevitable. Meadow Ed gladdened my heart by telling me that we were in no danger from other hikers.

"Who's going to walk 30 miles carrying 30 pounds and still have the energy for sex?"

Blithely I took this in and later re-told it to Staggering Willy, laughing heartily. He didn't laugh. He chewed a piece of grass and said;

"Well . . . ."

But even so things were relaxed—within half an hour of meeting we were both skinny-dipping in the river. It may sound raunchy back in Blighty with the rain pouring down on the window panes, and enough clothes on to hibernate a family of squirrels, but in California when you're sweaty and dirty and there's no chance of a shower for another week then you see things slightly differently. And it's not like anyone's going to carry a swimming costume and towel. Gene shrugged his shoulders and told me some story about a German girl (the implication being 'these Europeans') and Hobbit was equally unconcerned. They had all done long-distance hikes before and for them it was standard procedure.

Day Two out with Vive and we came to our first stream. The day before had been scaldingly hot with a big climb and as I seemed to be the only hiker carrying deodorant, a wash didn't seem like a bad idea. I put my sarong on and lowered myself into the water, unwrapping as I went in.

"NO!" shouted Vive.

"What?" I asked in concern, turning round, thinking a great disaster had befallen us.

He had one hand covering his eyes, and the other held out in protest. "NO!"

"Um, I'm just washing, really, it's ok."

I gave up and just splashed the water over my body underneath the sarong.

We walk together, chatting. I stop to pee. Vive stops.

"Vive, I'm going to pee."

"Oh," and he moves 20 feet or so and waits.

This is a very different experience for me. Gene and Hobbit each just did their own thing and we happened to arrive at some point to camp together or not. Staggering Willy and I walked the best together, crossing each other every few hours. Even with Kris it wasn't quite like this. At first we walked some 200 yards apart. Then later, when relations had disintegrated and I got bored of waiting for her to be ready in the morning, we walked separately, meeting every so often at water or for breaks. When Vive walks behind I feel like I'm not going fast enough so I walk faster and then he walks faster to catch up. When he walks ahead he goes too slow. It all seems very petty but walking at your own pace is one of the most important things to do as a thru-hiker. Out for a week or a few days and it doesn't really matter, but day after day walking too slow or too fast is exhausting.

One evening we met a south-bounder who said, "So *you're* Natasha."

I was puzzled and the south-bounder was mysterious.

"You'll see, there's something up ahead."

Kris, who has now arrived in Canada, had met up with some people including Turtle. (Yes! Turtle is still going!) He has been leaving me messages since then along the lines of 'catch up!' but it's a bit the case of me being the tortoise and Turtle the hare. So Vive, who hiked with Turtle and two women called Lora and Kadiddle through the Sierras, and I surmised that probably Turtle was at work again.

Two days out of Ashland, getting tired in the evening, and suddenly up in front is a white box taped at eye-level to a tree with ribbons dangling from it. It reads in large letters:

For Natasha from England, Trail Angel

Now I'm really puzzled. No hiker could have left a box, who else do I know? Inside the box which the jays/woodpeckers had attempted and failed to discover were some treats—jerky, sweets, an energy drink, crackers and a hand-crafted 'woodsman story weaver' doll.

Do you remember the women chopping at the tree trying to get their horses through the trail? And the trail crew who I thought were rather reluctant to go back up to them? Well obviously they came to the rescue and the two managed to finish their ride. This was a thank you from Brenda and Diane. Thank **you**! We stayed the night in a cross-country ski shelter, had a fire and feasted. What a wonderful surprise.

This was my first night in a shelter. Unlike the AT, which has shelters every ten miles or so, the PCT has virtually none. There is a beautiful round stone hut on top of Muir Pass, but it is an emergency shelter and to stay the night would have meant walking through the snow at its worst time of day—late in the afternoon when it is slushy, and early in the morning when it is icy and dangerous. The perfect time for snowfields is about 11 o'clock in the morning when the snow is soft enough to cut footsteps, but crisp and crunchy enough for those footsteps to hold.

So with some delight we laid our sleeping bags out on the

shelves. This was a new shelter, complete with a stove and logs cut for the fire. Perfect. There was even a pump just behind some bushes outside. Taking care not to be seen this time, I hastily tried to wash as the bees buzzed around the water. Since the washing incident on the second day, I have been a little more modest which has not been too difficult as this is a fairly dry section—gone are the daily leaps into lakes and creeks.

Nothing is good in Vive's life and he's very happy about that. His eyebrows are pure Labrador and he takes me through his aches and pains with a forlorn '*but-what-can-you-do?*' look. One lunchtime, following the washing incident, he announced:

"Lora and Kadiddle—they called me 'The Babe'."

I'm duly stunned.

"The Babe?"

"Yeah," he grins.

"Something to do with sheep and a pig?"

"No, no, 'The Babe', you know, as in, well, you know."

"No."

"I mean, I know I'm not classically what you would call a 'Babe', but . . . ."

He proceeds with several stories. There was the time when Kadiddle said no way could he get a ride so he walked into the road and three women wearing bikinis and sun-hats in an open-topped saloon pulled up.

"On the hike?" I question, a little incredulous.

"Yes! Just after the Sierras."

"What did you do?"

"Well, I mean, I couldn't get in, could I? I told them to go on, I'd get another ride."

"Are you making this up?"

"No, no! It was awful!"

Not every man's idea of awful. Then there was the one about the masseuse who pinned him down and forced him to succumb to a back massage given, rather unusually, from the front, and then the one about an old lady who picked him up and spent the whole day driving him around wherever he wanted to go.

"I mean, I could have killed her, she was just a little old lady," says Vive.

Vive

Shortly after dark and sleeping time we were woken by the very small sound of plastic moving.

"Vive?" I say.

"It's not me," says Vive.

He shines his light and a mouse scurries away along the shelf. I have my food safe beside me, Vive's is in his pack on the floor. (Um, kind of given up on the bears—it's a three-sided shelter, no logic, just couldn't be bothered that night.)

"What did we leave over there?"

Neither of us want to crawl out into the cold unless it's to rescue something important.

"Nothing," says Vive.

We sleep again.

Crackle, crackle, crackle.

"Tasha?" says Vive.

"It's not me," I say.

I throw something in the direction of the noise and the mouse scuttles away.

Sleep again.

Crackle, crackle, crackle.

"Mouse go away!"

I got up to see what it was trying to eat and discovered the 'woodman story weaver' doll, thankfully still in one piece, and some plastic bags chewed to bits.

Day 127—1825.3 trail miles north
Mazama

Oregon is notorious for mosquitoes, all the guide books talk of them, all the hikers, everyone. Oregon = rain, mosquitoes and trees. However, I am walking through Oregon later than most of the hikers/ guide book writers—the worst must be over, I had my mosquito time in California, it can't possibly happen again, can it? Please no. Day Four in Oregon and we're taking a break. (I stop, Vive stops;

"You don't have to stop," say I.

"No, no, I'll stop," says Vive.)

I've got a sesame seed bar which requires a lot of physical energy just to chew. Hopefully it makes up for it in calories and protein. And then I hear the whine.

"What was that?"

"What?" says Vive.

I look down at my legs suspiciously, waiting to see something small and dark hovering ready to bite. Then the whine comes again.

"Mosquitoes," I say, full of dread. (It may have come out just a leettle bit dramatically.)

Vive looks at me, a little surprised and a little scornful.

"Just a bug or two," he says, digging up some seeds from a plastic bag into his finger tips. "They won't bother you."

"Oh, they bother me."

And I'm gone. Vive with finger tips and seeds poised just above his open mouth, looks slightly startled.

My next break is the same, I stop briefly until I hear the familiar whine. This time I spend a bit longer looking for the particular mosquito concerned. Where is it? It isn't until the next stop that I remembered that there were things here called 'no-see-ums' which, as their name would suggest, are not visible to the human eye. Thankfully they don't seem to bite either.

Day Six in Oregon, and it began to rain. Just lightly, nothing to worry about. A break from the sweltering heat. Day Seven and the rain was sleet. Day Eight we awoke to find the world white. Six inches of thick snow and a small herd of elk; Christmas card weather at the beginning of September. Not exactly dressed for the weather (me in shorts) after our 90 degrees plus sojourn in California, we stomped into Crater Lake, very wet and very cold. What was I saying about making it before winter? Maybe it's just a freak storm.

Snow

There we met the aforementioned legendary Scott 'Yo-yo' Williamson, who has just completed his fifth thru-hike of the PCT. This year he has had snow every month since he started back in April. Crazy! Washington could prove cold.

It took us three 'rides' to get in and out of Crater Lake Park and find our boxes. In one of the trucks I lost my tent-poles. Considering the weather this is not good. The first lift was me at the side of the road soaked through with squelchy ice-block feet looking my most forlorn in the rain—I actually mouth the word 'please' as the cars pass and look after them raising my hands in a gesture of despair. Don't laugh; this works. A couple once turned around 20 minutes further down the road and came back to pick me up. This time, Vive had left me and started walking, working on the theory that 'girls get a ride in seconds'. This was my second longest wait—about ten minutes and ten cars, probably because of the rain. The next lift was a couple that we both thought immediately 'they'll take us' and then the third a campground host.

Everyone has different theories. 'Never walk, people think you can get there' versus 'start walking, they think at least you're trying'. 'Wear your pack, it makes you look smaller and ready to go' versus 'hide your pack out of sight' versus 'stand in front of your pack so it looks small, but make sure they can see it so they know you're a hiker'. Of course none of this helps if there is no traffic.

Mum and Dad failed dismally to get from Seiad Valley, where they had parked the mobile home, back to Etna, where they were meeting up with me to walk the Marble Mountain Wilderness stretch of the PCT. Hitching for the first time in their lives—there was no public transport—they ended up after six hours calling on the fire service. Two officers took them 60 miles out of their way when they had finished work—nobody can say Americans aren't hospitable. On the same day, I arrived at Etna Summit and saw two guys and a dog—there's my ride, I thought. Sure enough they took me right down into Etna town and even offered to take me out to see their marijuana plantation:

"Hey Dude, you rock!"

Um, thanks.

One of them was a car mechanic and had moved specifically to Etna (a very small place) because of the high incident of accidents. As we flew round the corners down into the valley it was easy to see why. The most common occurrence is a collision with a deer. My 'dudes' had also seen three mountain lions in the last year on this road. They also told me about the local cult who wore long robes, clutched chains and sacrificed animals. (This turned out to be the Greek Orthodox Church who carried rosaries and kept goats.)

Today was a trip on the back of a Harley Davidson with a guy at the bikers' rally, after failing to get a ride in a horse-box with someone attending the local cow-pinning contest.

My first hitch terrified me. Now, with no shame, I smile like a daughter at each driver, whilst making sure to show a bit of leg. The worst hitch? Trying to get off the Sierras into Lone Pine, from a dead end. After an hour or so of no one, a father and daughter arrived on the scene returning after one night in the mountains because the bugs were too bad. I begged a lift in the two-seater saying, "Can I sit in the back with the dogs?" One of the friendly beasts took a chunk out of my arm as I climbed in—lost some T-shirt.

Day 128—1833.1 trail miles north
Crater Lake

Stuck. And frustrated. Still in Crater Lake. We stayed the night in a tepee—the cheapest thing available that wasn't our own wet gear—and then waited around on Sunday. Then on Monday we eventually got a lift back up to the lake and started plodding through the snow. Then the trail became too difficult so we dropped down to road walk. Then the snow started again and we thought, what the hell, let's hitch. Floyd, a fire-watchman picked us up and took us to the next junction with the PCT. We all sat round and ate lunch and then the skies opened.

"Come and have a piece of pie and a cup of tea," said Floyd.

So we agreed and sat in the Diamond Lake Resort while the weather came in thick and fast.

"Let's get a drink," said Floyd.

And we drank whisky as the lake, not 15 yards away, disappeared into a thick cloud.

"Come back and stay," said Floyd. "Leave warm and dry in the morning."

As Vive says, Trail Angels always turn up when you need them. So back to where we arrived on Saturday, spaghetti and Scrabble with Floyd. Floyd watches for fires for a living, as Jack Kerouac did for a summer. He stands posted in the hut on top of The Watchman—an 8056 foot peak of lava flow above Crater Lake— and looks out over the mass of forest below him.

"How do you know when it's smoke and not fog?" we ask.

"You get to tell," says Floyd. "Fog clears within a few minutes, smoke grows bigger."

I recalled the mile or two of smouldering trail in Northern California.

"You remember," I said to Vive, "before Castella, there was this cliff top path and a whole side of newly burnt trees."

"No," says Vive, "when I went through there was no burn at all."

I found out later that two hikers called Madame Butterfly and Improv who I never met but whose imprints I followed religiously for several hundred miles, had actually come across the fire and hiked off-trail to notify the authorities.

Tuesday morning and the road is closed. We are sitting by the fire in the lodge not sure what to do. Walk out? Wait? Are we being feeble?

The highlight of all this to-ing and fro-ing was driving back around Crater Lake with the fog rolling in around us, the fresh snow gleaming in the sunset and the cold blue water glittering below. Crater Lake is the deepest lake in the U.S. The sides of this volcanic crater sweep 900 feet down to the water which then plunges a further 1932 feet to its depths. It is haughty and grand and very spectacular—the end result of the massive eruption of Mount Mazama in 4900 BC as recorded by the Klamath people.

Crater Lake

Day 130—1886.4 trail miles north
Lake Pinewan

Finally did manage to leave Crater Lake and chomp through the snow around Mount Thielsen. Now several thousand feet lower, it is hot again, blue lakes and pine forests. The bugs have gone and been replaced by bees—thin wasp-like bees. I hate wasps. Maybe even more than I hate mosquitoes. Vive sits relaxed in his T-shirt and boxer-shorts (thinking the good weather had gone he sent his shorts away and only has black GoLite trousers to walk in) munching away on his lunch. I huddle in bug-proof clothing, snatching a mouthful every now and then before running round in a circle. Vive shakes his head patronisingly. We have arrived, very quickly, at a bantering relationship. I hassle, nag, jibe and tease, and Vive sighs his sighs and gasps his gasps and says 'I'm so hard done by!' in every look and comment.

"Lora and Kadiddle, they were just the same, they picked on me just like you: pick, pick, pick."

"You love it!"

"Pick, pick, pick."

Kris made a valiant effort to be able to recognise all the different types of pine trees: ponderosa pine, pinyon pine, digger pine, sugar pine, Jeffrey pine, lodge-pole pine, western white pine, white bark pine, foxtail pine, knobcone pine, Coulter pine, limber pine. Not to be confused with Douglas fir, white fir, grand fir, red fir, Shasta red fir, noble fir, western juniper or incense cedar.

I can hardly even begin. All have different leaf and bark combinations. Ponderosa pines have barks like jigsaw puzzles, foxtail pines have tufts of leaves like foxtails, western white pines do have white-ish trunks, but then so do sugar pines. And all red firs are kind of red.

Right now it's lodge-pole pine, that's easy: tall and straight as, well, lodge-poles. The almost branchless trees soar upwards leaving the forest floor still and silent. Above, the wind rushes through the tops and half-fallen trunks crack like old pirate ships. With the mist blowing off the gloomy green lakes, Oregon is eerie. A pale green string moss has attacked patches of forest, hanging heavily off the dying branches like witches' hair. Enough, I'm writing a ghost story.

More disturbing was a moth in the Klamath Valley area, that spins webs around the maple and madrone trees, leaving them encased in a thick binding of sticky white. Inside hundreds of caterpillars crawl back and forth munching their way through the tree.

"Pick, pick, pick."

It's been nice to have company. I've come out of my cocoon, socialised, played a role for a week, now I'm tired of it. Subtleties are lost out here.

"Shall we go?" Vive might say.

"I'm going to hang around for a bit, I'll see you there," I say, meaning yes, let's take some space from each other.

"Oh, I'll wait," says Vive.

"No, really you don't have to, please go on."

"No, it's fine, I'll wait."

I should just skip the formality and be direct, but it's hard to go against upbringing. Instead, I gobble lunch, leap up and run (Vive's natural pace is slower than mine, so if I get ahead I can stay ahead). There's a junction and I glance at it and stride onwards as it begins to rain. Back in my own dream world I can relax again, be me, be unadulterated me. There is no-one to please, no-one to keep happy, no-one to play a certain role for, no-one to be responsible for, no-one who feels responsible for me. Back in my own little world of self-sufficiency, I walk on as the rain gets heavier and enjoy the simple pleasure of walking.

Two hours later I decide to take a short break, and choose a trail junction—Vive is not likely to stop before that and from here I will see him coming. Twenty minutes later there is no sign of him and it's really raining. I am getting cold. Gone is my thick five dollar Canadian 'Mickey Mouse' fleece and gone is my big Gore-Tex jacket. Instead I have, from my mother, light weight replacements—a thin fleece and a cagoule. When taken to extremes the travelling light ideology requires you to keep moving in bad weather. Scott the Yo-yo was going so light that he had to eat in the middle of the night in order to warm up. Now that's extreme. I do not want to end up with hypothermia and decide to move on. I walk another ten minutes and stop for a while, then another and so on. There is no sign of Vive. What can have happened to him?

Should I go back? Is he in trouble? It's not like we're hiking partners—if it was Kris I would be in no doubt and go back, but hikers who just meet up on the trail have no immediate responsibility towards one another. Willee Color for instance never showed up and if I had gone to look for him it would have been all the way back to Sierra City only to find out that he'd left the trail. The 'see you down the trail' with which hikers take leave of each other, is as non-committal as it gets. See you down the trail if you happen to show up in the same place where I am, or walk at the same speed. But with Vive? I am sure he wouldn't just not show up. I'm thinking all this as I walk along in the pouring rain. If I go back the five or six miles I'll have to camp there, that's ten miles extra walking. It will get dark soon and I'm cold, tired and wet. Ahead is a lake where we've vaguely mentioned we'll camp. I decide to go to there, get a fire going and see what happens.

At the junction to the lake someone has left a message—a hiker kind of message, scrap paper in a zip-lock bag. I have left a few messages myself, one was a massive '*VEG FOREVER*' written in pine cones to say hi to the Menacing Vegetables. The note is from Vive. '*I'm down here*', it says, with an arrow pointing.

What? How?

Vive, speeding along to catch up with me, glanced at the first junction and took the wrong turning. Ended up walking towards Portland. He didn't realise until he was several miles down the trail and came to a dirt road that was not on the map. Whilst he was pondering his mistake, a ranger showed up in a jeep and drove him to the lake. He has the fire going. Sometimes it's very good to be bugged.

I strung my tent up using my long bear rope and still had enough to throw the rest over a tree to hang my food. I'm getting quite good at constructing shelter without tent poles. Vive has a tarp and mentions the benefits each night. Vive is very much of the GoLite philosophy and has the clothes as well as the tarp—it's a great needle to tease him with, though I think he gets as much mileage from me for not having the equipment. It's a big tarp and he has offered me space inside, but I'm actually quite enjoying having to find, and experiment with, different methods of putting up the fly or body of my tent minus the poles. The first night without the poles I used sticks—criss-crossed in a three-pronged tepee style at the front, and the same at the back, and then draped the fly over the top. It was very effective, but extremely difficult to get in and out of and useless if you happen to be a night time kicker or thrasher. Yesterday, it didn't look like rain and I just tied up the body of the tent. Now I have pegged the bottom end of the fly to the ground and used the rope to hold the top end up, and then pegged down the sides. It seems relatively good. The advantage of Vive's is that you can eat underneath without getting wet (I can't sit up inside my shelter). Vive eats and sleeps with his food (stupid). I eat where he sleeps (sensible) and then hang my food. He shows no inclination to worry about bears, which is fine by me.

We arrived at Shelter Cove Resort where my tent poles were meant to be waiting. It was a fishing resort—a lake and a few wooden cabins. The woman at the reception/shop was decidedly unfriendly.

"We've written to the PCT for the last THREE years, we DON'T pick up parcels any more. They only come here if you send them U.P.S." she said.

"So where would our packages be?"

"How should I know? Crescent Lake. In the valley. 12 mile hitch."

We ate a hot dog each and debated what to do. I phoned the post office to see what had arrived. Two packages for Vive, two packages for me. That meant the food box from Kris, my old backpack sent back from my sister-in-law Anna Marie (the one from my mother was proving not nearly as comfortable despite the fact that it weighed less) but no tent poles. I would have to wait until tomorrow.

As the post office opened at eight in the morning we decided to hitch down that night, get some serious food (lots of it) and stay down there so we could be up and out as soon as possible the next day. So we showered and washed clothes and then hitched into town for the evening. 'Town' turned out to be a 200-yard strip along the highway. Opposite the post office, where we gathered the boxes that had already arrived, was a certain establishment called Manley's Tavern. It was a heavy low-ceilinged barn built of long dark planks of tree, with booths, pool-tables and the kind of décor that so many British bars attempt to imitate. In Britain you end up with fake light wood

panelled on to the walls and cheesy American licence plates
hanging next to fake moose-heads. Parents grumble into their
all-American food whilst the kids flick oversized croutons from
the Caesar salad across the check gingham tablecloth. In Crescent
Lake Junction, however, the 'real McCoy' was somewhat
different. The solid door showed conspicuous evidence that it
had been driven into more than once in its lifetime, probably
by something significantly larger than a European Smart Car;
the windows were grilled, presumably to stop the damage of
flying glass. The silent atmosphere spoke volumes. We sat in
our booth and ordered the usual humongous plates of food so
large they take up the entire table. The pool playing was shifty
and serious. The lights hung above each table rendering the
watching players to the shadows. No-one spoke. And all this
with no smoking and no drinking of hard liquor (beer or cider
only). Jesus.

At about ten o'clock Vive and I left, heaved our backpacks
on, picked up our boxes and looked left and right. Time for
stealth-camping. Stealth-camping is something Ray Jardine is
an expert on. Ray and Jenny stealth-camp every night, even in
the wilderness. They wander off-trail several miles after eating
their evening meal and find a spot on a slight gradient (in
order that the blood might drain from the feet during the night)
and, with the minimum of impact and noise, sleep the night
hidden in the undergrowth. Jardine's book has a whole chapter
devoted to the subject and it does make a good deal of sense,
environmentally if nothing else. Stealth-camping in a town,
however, is for entirely different motives—namely not wanting
to pay extortionate rates for nasty noisy accommodation. I am
keen to try again after my last unsuccessful attempt in
Tuolumne with the bear and ranger. We crossed the highway
and walked into the forest in the darkness away from the lights
of the bar and garage.

"How about here?" Vive whispered.

"No, further, someone might see us."

We picked a spot and quickly found the ground was littered

with glass bottles—this was obviously where the serious drinking went on in Crescent Lake Junction.

"Hmm, say the men come out here when the bar closes?"

Vive grunted and proceeded to lay out his groundsheet. I arranged my boxes and backpack around me and tied the straps underneath my mat and back around my camera—a practice I had got into in Southern California when I was convinced someone would happen upon us in the night and steal it. (I hadn't quite comprehended the sheer size of the U.S. at that point. Only two per cent of the country is built up, so it's really not that likely a thief would happen upon you in the wilderness.) I lay down for a while amongst the glass bottles and food containers. This place must be rat heaven. My mind started wondering back to the drinkers—what would happen if they came across us? Got to save my camera. So I untied it from the straps and hid it in the clump of a tree a few feet away. Lay down again. Would rats get my food? Should I hang it up? I sat up again. Vive sighed.

"What are you doing?" he asked wearily.

So I started explaining to him my theories of drinking men, cameras and rats, calmly I should say, with logic.

Vive sat up.

"Do you think we should move?"

"Oh, no," I said, laying back down again, "I'm just preparing for every eventuality."

"It's all right for you!" says Vive. "You're just a girl, I'm the one who'll get beaten up!"

There was a pause, while I digested this.

"Right."

"I mean it! I could be killed!" he said, whispering furiously. "They're going to leave me for dead!"

"Vive, it's all right, I'll call for help or something, we're probably on private property anyway, there's a house over there."

"A house? Oh shit, now we're going to get shot!"

He leapt to his feet still dressed in his boxer shorts and pale green T-shirt with 'NEVER SAY DIE' written in goofy writing across the front and large sweat patches beneath the arms (he had asked his sister to send him a replacement—luminous yellow with a psychedelic pattern on the front but it hadn't arrived yet) and began staring at the ground and turning in circles.

"Vive, I'll call the sheriff, it will be all right."

"The sheriff?" his voice cracked, "The sheriff? I'm going to be beaten up, shot at and then deported! I won't even be able to finish the hike!"

By this time he was packing his things, muttering all the while about being pulverised just because he wasn't a GIRL and it wasn't his fault and . . . . Eventually, for want of anywhere better to go, Vive lay down again and all was quiet apart from the roar of trucks passing along Highway 58. Not, however, the best night's sleep.

That's the last time I go stealth-camping.

Day 133—1944.3 trail miles north
Cliff Lake Shelter

It is mushroom season. The serious mushroomers are out looking for pine-mushrooms, which grow bigger than saucers and are used in ceremonies in Japan. The best lie still covered by the pine needles, nothing visible but a slight hump. At 600 dollars a pound these mushrooms are well worth defending. Hikers straying from the trail have been known to receive warning shots.

So now we're past the two-week bow and arrow buck-hunting season and the two-week rifle-hunting season, we have to handle the mushroom season and then the elk season. The deer hunters are the most bizarre. They turn up in full-leaf camouflage, wearing outfits that look like they belong next to the Superman and Batman costumes on the eight-year-olds' rack at Woolworth's. You have to question the need when a hiker singing songs and with a bright red pack, can stomp up to within 15 feet of the deer.

Population sprawl and hunting have diminished the number of mountain lions, which in turn has meant a boom in deer numbers. The only problem with hunting as a method of control is that the mountain lions would choose the older weaker specimens whereas the hunters go for those in their prime.

Day 135—1984.2 trail miles north
McKenzie Pass

Vive has just gone into town and I am instantly lonely. Perhaps I should have gone too. But the urge to keep moving; I feel guilty when I stop. Still that drive, that urgency to walk walk walk. I miss it instantly, and the mountains. Coming down to a road and you get that awful feeling of hurry hurry, let me come back soon. Miss that beautiful peace and the comfort of being alone. Town-stops are lonely. Mountains are alone.

Rain one day, bright the next. We managed to find the occasional three-sided shelter to hide from the Scottish-like weather, but none quite like the first one. Everyone said that the trail through Oregon was boring and flat. It is relatively level, but also beautiful. Wandering through the mist across the plains, struggling across lava flows, river-crossing where the water is white from the glacier silt and the shine of obsidian gleaming black from the ground. Three Sisters' Wilderness. I love it.

Worst mile? The last one, across a lava field—tedious and crippling.

Best mile? Muir Pass for scenic value, every step into icy knee-deep snow, finding your own trail was a thrill.

As they were being chased out of their homeland, the Modoc people hid in lava fields like this a little further south from here. Wearing sage brush in their head-dresses, a band of 51 managed to outwit the volunteer and regular troops, suffering not one casualty while the other side was heavily depleted. I cannot imagine how they managed to move and function so well in this environment—I find it difficult even walking along the trail. 'Land of Burnt-out Fires' the Modocs called it. Sounds far too nice for the sharp black cobbled lava that makes my feet scream out with each step.

The tent pole saga is ongoing. Anna Marie has become an additional member of the support crew (along with Kris and her parents who are sending out re-supply boxes). Anna Marie managed to get new poles express-mailed to me, but unfortunately the store sent the wrong poles. Find-a-telephone-time. Oregon is, perhaps not unsurprisingly, lacking in wilderness telephones. Wet, but walking well, we took a lunch break a few days ago, off-trail at Elk Lake Resort. Five dollars a minute for the telephone. And that's to phone a free-phone number. I used one minute and one second, and yes, the bill came to ten dollars. Ouch. The trouble with many of these 'town-stops'— three houses can make a town in the States—is that you are in the middle of nowhere and they have you. Most of them make up for it in friendliness and hospitality like the excellent Vermilion Valley Resort whose owners made everyone feel at home. Elk Lake, however, really took the piss.

Today I arrived at Big Lake Youth Camp where they were closing up for the season. The kids had all gone, the camps were over, and Eric and Donavan were preparing for the annual 14 foot of snow (Wow! That covers most of the buildings. Maybe I should start running.) Donavan kindly lent me his mobile and I called Anna Marie briefly—a tent is on its way! They showed me the boat that Eric is building and said,

"Have you ever been sailing?"

"No."

"Well, let's go then."

With that I gave up any notion of moving on and we took the catamaran out and flew across the water.

Early evening and a couple called Celest and Steve turned up. So we went water-skiing while the sun set on the red Mount Washington and then watched a movie. This has been my best rest time yet.

Tomorrow I cross the 2000-mile marker. Then the count down starts. For the first time in months, I really feel like I might make it.

Day 137—2015.5 trail miles north
Rockpile Lake

There was no marker at 2000 miles but I stopped at roughly the right place and Steve snapped a photo.

Me at 2000 miles

2000 miles was our original target. Now if I want to, I have full licence to stop, give up. Got to walk out to Olallie at least. I camped with Steve and Celest at Rockpile Lake and they pointed out the Great Pacific Salamanders, which have disproportionately large heads and gills making them look like the babies of a Hollywood-style monster. Steve and Celest are section-hiking Oregon in their holidays from work on an estuary and hope to hike the whole trail next year.

As a European it is very easy to forget just how recent non-native American history is. And one thing that brings it back with a shock each time is names. In Britain most of our place names date back to Roman times (Winchester, Chichester) or to Saxon words which we no longer understand (Crondall, Itchel). There are some Amerindian names left here too which no doubt date back further: Tipsoo Peak, Suiattle Pass, Siskiyou, Yakima. But there are also more modern treasures such as Lipstick Lake, Fryingpan Mountain, Cement Bluffs, Doodlebug Gulch, the Nip & Tuck

Lakes, Telephone Lake, Tinker Knob. Some of Northern California was 'discovered' as recently as 150 years ago. I am crossing many of the same routes with which those travellers attempted to 'Go West'. And sometimes you wonder what happened on those 'Go West' journeys to give rise to Deadman Creek or Bloody Run Trail. Then there is the descriptive collection: Bend, A Tree (only it was forested—which was the original tree?), Gobber's Knob (what exactly did they do there?) or my favourite, The Nipple.

I was with Staggering Willy when we first saw The Nipple on the map. We managed to poke our heads up briefly above the trees and saw ahead what could only be The Nipple—a nice gentle rounded nipple, fair enough, good description. As we got closer and closer however, this hump turned out to be altogether in the wrong place, not directly north as it was on the map. This lovely soft mound with its delicately pointed tip was not The Nipple and instead, horror of horrors, a ragged jagged sharp-toothed spiky rock on a ragged jagged steep-sided hill was *The Nipple*. Those early Americans must have experienced some bad nipples.

Thundering down into Olallie Lake I came across someone in front of me, scouring the bushes for signs of ripe purple huckleberries (Olallie means huckleberry in one of the native languages from here). Most likely a weekender. I started by asking a few summary questions.

"Out here for long?"

"Oh, a while. You?"

"Yeah, a while."

(Thru-hikers never give away too much information.)

"Heading in to Olallie?"

"Yeah, going to re-supply there."

"Oh yeah? Me too."

(Only thru-hikers or section-hikers talk of re-supplying.)

"Where did you start?"

"Oh, um Mexico."

"A thru-hiker!"

(And then it's easy.)

"How're the feet?"

"Yeah, not so bad. Yours?"

"Good good."

(Thru-hikers talk about feet in the way that the British talk about the weather.)

"Back?"

"Couple of twinges, nothing serious."

"Want some nuts?"

"Got my own thanks. Swap you a Mars bar for something though."

"Mars bar? Sure, I've got a couple of Power bars."

"Ooh, don't know if I can eat any more of them."

"They got hot food at Olallie?"

"Oh yes please. Could murder a veggie-burger."

(Conversations like this can go on for several hours, days even.)

"I'm, err, Seven Grains."

"Is there a story?"

(There usually is.)

"My food, I read Jardine and I've got this seven grain meal that I eat."

"Oh, bad luck."

We stomped into Olallie—an empty ranger station and a fishing shop—which is not exactly on the highway. There was a familiar figure sitting swinging mournfully on a hammock.

"Hey Vive!"

"Hi," said Vive, dolefully and looking even more glum than usual.

"This is Glen."

(Glen is about as au fait with his trail name as I am with mine.)

"Hi, Glen," says Vive, the eyebrows rising to heights of despair.

Glen and I went to investigate any food possibilities (a microwave and some frozen burritos—yum yum yum) and pick up our parcels. Glen it turns out started in Mexico but on the Continental Divide Trail. The CDT is the third and most challenging big trail through the States. It runs 3000 miles through New Mexico, Colorado, Wyoming, Idaho and Montana, and has still to be mapped in some of the states. Glen was forced off when he got to Yellowstone due to the raging fires—pretty much the whole state of Montana is on fire at the moment and they have a State of Emergency. So he decided to move across country and finish walking to Canada on a different trail.

The usual discussion followed about who's staying, who's moving on. We're all always moving on, and we all always end up staying. It turned out to be Vive's birthday (is that why the long face?) and the lady from the fishing shop offered him a free room in the boat house. We gathered some edible supplies, some beer to celebrate, and a few extra hikers—Steve and Celest turned up along with a veteran hiker called Let-it-be and his dog going southbound, and set up camp in the boat house. Bears and Ray Jardine dominated the conversation, until we got on to Vive.

Vive passed me when I was at Big Lake Youth Camp and then took an alternate route. One day he sat down on a log to have his lunch. There were a few wasps flying around but he brushed them away and pulled out his pot, and started heating some water. There seemed to be a few more wasps and they seemed to be getting a bit more angry. He added the dried stuffing mix to the water. The wasps got considerably worse. He stood up and suddenly noticed that the log was hollow and swarming with wasps. He ran, abandoning not only his lunch, but also his pack and its contents. Quarter of a mile down the trail, Vive started creeping back. There was no doubt, the wasps had control of his log, his lunch and his pack. He crept gingerly forward, dived in and grabbed the nearest thing and ran down the trail again. He now had ownership once again of a ziplock bag full of salt. Great. The same operation went on several times and he eventually managed to regain his pack and belongings but at the cost of several wasp stings. He set off down the trail, no doubt feeling rather traumatised by the whole experience. A while later he met two guys out just returning from a day-hike. He told them about the wasps and one of them mentioned the possibility of allergic reactions. Vive instantly fell prey. He needed medicine, care and attention. They took him down off-trail and drove him to a chemist where he picked up some drugs. He now explained that he was still feeling rather strange due to the wasp stings.

"How many of these drugs did you take Vive?" asks Celest, holding up the packet.

"I don't know, I wanted to get better you know, five or six."

"'Not to be consumed with alcohol'," she read from the back of the packet.

We all collapsed with laughter. I am very glad that wasn't me—I probably would have had to abandon my pack.

Bees can actually be quite a problem in Oregon. Sometimes you can get used to them landing on everything as you cook and eat and if you manage to stay relaxed enough they don't sting. One time there was a note lying on the trail. In scrawly writing it said *'Caution Bees Nest—100 yards ahead'*. Then in 50 yards there was another; *'Caution Bees Nest—50 yards ahead'*, and then 30, 20 and so on, until finally the last one which read *'RUN! NOW!'* I followed the instructions and ran for 20 yards or so. There was a big hole right on the trail, but I saw no bees—probably they all emerged angrily after I had run by and picked on the next hiker.

Day 140—2068.7 trail miles north
Warm Springs River

It's lunchtime. Vivek, who has been fairly silent since our somewhat mute reunion at Olallie Lake, says that he wants to ask my advice about something.

"What?"

He prefers not to mention it in the company of others (Glen, myself and Vive are sitting beneath a tree eating lunch—Steve and Celest ended their holiday and hike in Olallie with plans to walk the whole trail next year.) Can he talk while we hike? He knows he has to ask permission for this because I have made it quite clear that 'I hike alone!' (Pick, pick, pick; Bug, bug, bug.)

"Of course," I say, speculating on what he could possibly want advice about from me—his next town-stop? His bee stings? His chafing? His ankle? (He fell over this morning, but happily in front of an old lady who gave him some apples and brownies.)

Lunch ends and we start hiking, me in front, Vive behind. He says something about going into Portland and makes general chit-chat.

"What Vive, what?" I ask, anxious to get into my own rhythm, to re-enter my daydream world.

And then it dawns on me. It should have clicked instantly, but I'm smelly, dirty, my hair—unwashed since April—is greasy. How desperate can he be?

"I met this girl a couple of weeks ago," begins Vive.

'Chrysalis' starts walking slightly faster,

" . . . and we're just good friends . . ."

It's uphill, but faster and faster we go,

" . . . but every time I see her . . ."

In between the pants for breath, while I speed-walk up the hill, Vive struggles to declare his undying love.

Time to move on, methinks.

Day 143—2132.1 trail miles north 7½ mile camp

We walked around Mount Hood in a state of some awe, partly because of the barren, glaciated channels of water, but mostly because of the modern day myth of *The Shining*. Mount Hood is home to Timberline Lodge where some of the filming of the scary effects of cabin fever supposedly took place. Just on the other side of the mountain, after crossing the gouged-out gorges made of volcanic glaciated dust, we came across a tarp strung across the trail. The occupants were still in bed, giggling. Turtle! I'm delighted to see Turtle. But Turtle has been hiking with a girl called Lora for some time and they now constitute the trail romance, going 'relationship pace' as Vive later commented (i.e. they stay in bed all day). Still, I'm glad he's walking. Hope he makes it. Turtle and Lora were meant to be meeting Lora's brother in Cascade Locks that evening. It was midday when we met them and we were about

30 miles from town. Just ahead was Lolo Pass where there are a few roads and with any luck maybe some traffic. They had decided to hitch. Vive quickly chose to stay with them, and I set off to pursue Glen, but with my feet the way they are there was not much hope of catching him up. Back to little old me.

I plodded on through clear-cuts where the huckleberry bushes and ferns were above waist-height and heavy with rain. My trousers were quickly soaked, the uphill seemed exhausting and everything was damp and cold. I caught up with Glen who was waiting at the turn off to the alternate route down Eagle Creek Falls Trail. We cooked and ate and then said goodbye—Glen reckoned he would make it all the way to town, or close enough to stroll a few miles tomorrow.

Onwards.

The detour had no qualms about breaking the PCT gradient and the path plunged down through the forest. At first I leapt and bounded enjoying the difference. Then I hobbled and longed for my poles.

Resolve is breaking down.

Time to sing. Sing loudly against the noise of the crashing water that gets louder and louder with each bend. Eventually the path joined the river and there was a small space of even ground. Time to camp. I untied my laces and strung up my tent. Hobbled down to the water and washed my face. Sat and ate humous on a rock.

If there was a road I would hitch right now.

Feet hurt so much, just about ready to drop.

Can someone please tell me to stop?

Stop now. Go home.

It's seven miles into town. Seven miles and I get to the Oregon/Washington border. I've walked far enough now. My feet hurt. Seven miles along the rocky path of Eagle Creek Falls Trail. This is a detour but one worth doing. The water pours down through all sorts of channels and tunnels, the highlight being a *Last of the Mohicans* moment where the trail passes behind a 50 foot waterfall in amongst the green hanging moss. The guide book suggests 'a *quick invigorating frolic'* in one of the pools below the fall (who are these people?) but I have never felt less like frolicking, quick or otherwise.

Only 500 miles to go. Across the Bridge of the Gods and into Washington State.

500 miles.

The home straight.

Stop.

WASHINGTON

WINTER WEATHER

Day 144—2150.3 trail miles north
Bridge of the Gods

Purists are people who want to walk every step of the Pacific Crest Trail. When they step off-trail for whatever reason, they make sure to step back on-trail at exactly the same point. They do not believe in alternative routes. They do not believe in slack-packing. Many do not even believe in water caches and think that Trail Angels are demons in disguise trying to lure hikers away from their goal.

I am, evidently, proudly and firmly, *not* a purist. Trail Angels, for one, are definitely angelic people who make the whole experience special. I am still amazed each time someone opens their door to me, drives me somewhere, gives me food. I have a feeling that the English would not be nearly as hospitable and friendly. Water caches are lifelines and walking without a pack is heavenly. I am also very happy to stray off-trail to an alternate route, especially if it has something of interest like the Devil's Postpile at Red's Meadows, a hot spring, or the scenic Eagle Creek Falls Trail.

I did, however, want to walk all the way from Mexico to Canada by whatever path was appropriate. It hasn't quite worked out like that. There were two miles missed through Agua Dulce, but they were road miles and I'm not here to road walk, I thought. Likewise coming into Seiad Valley, another few miles. These seemed unimportant. Then there was Crater Lake: 13 miles, but the weather was severe—whiteout conditions—so that seemed sensible.

Now, however, I have truly overstepped the line. I got a ride. Walk 35 miles, and climb 5000 feet and then drop back down again in the fog, or get a lift? Well I chose the latter and at the end of the day, who cares? No-one knows exactly how many miles the trail is anyway—seeing as the *Data Book* is different from the guide book is different from the monument at the start is different from the monument at the finish. And if anyone is counting miles what about all those many extra ones for water and into towns?

All I can say is I've walked bloody miles! And that's far enough.

I've met several Washingtonians who keep telling me, "You're in God's country now!" with a beaming smile on their faces. I don't know whether they consider Oregon to be shockingly heathen or whether they are referring to the legend surrounding the Bridge of the Gods. Amerindian mythology tells the story of how the land came down to form a natural bridge over the mighty Columbia River in order for the people to cross, and modern geography agrees quite happily. One of the writers of the guide book is a fanatical geologist and given the opportunity will wax lyrical about every pebble the PCT hiker steps on or over. For details you can see the book but the gist is that the upper layers of the lower level (being older and weaker) often collapse causing massive landslides that could well have been big enough to block the entire river.

Vive and I left Cascade Locks and (in a car) crossed the Bridge of the Gods with Turtle and Lora, but managed to lose them the very next day on the way to White Pass. Or rather they managed to lose us. Then we climbed up and around Mount Adams with views of the spectacular Mount Rainier and Mount St. Helens.

Once upon a time there was a great spirit called Klickitat, the totem-maker. Klickitat reigned over a vast region of valleys and hills, but on the edge of his territory lived another great spirit named Wyeast, the singer. Klickitat and Wyeast, knowing they were two of a kind, kept their distance from each other so as not to quarrel and reveal their less appealing sides. One day a young beauty appeared as if from nowhere, close by to Klickitat. Klickitat was mighty pleased and set about planning on how best to approach the spirit, aiming to woo her with a variety of methods. Wyeast, knowing nothing of Klickitat's feelings and

*unsure of any social techniques, charged headlong into the
adventure of love and instantly the two knew they had found a
soul mate in each other. Klickitat was furious: he loved the
Squaw and therefore she was his. And so the two great spirits
fought bitterly. Klickitat won, and Wyeast turned away in the
other direction to look on pastures new and relationships less
fraught. The Squaw was miserable and rejected all approaches
from Klickitat. Over time, their flames of desire burnt out and
their hatred turned them cold and barren. And this is the story
of Mount Adams (Klickitat), Mount Hood (Wyeast) and Mount
St. Helens (Squaw Mountain).*

Pacific Northwest[14]

St. Helens blew her top on 18th May, 1980, presumably because
she'd had enough of the whole damn business. People here
remember the coating of ash that covered everything and the dirt
which stayed for days after the eruption.

It's easy to say Kris should have left ages before she did. To walk
two months and 600 miles with a bad tendon was crazy. Why didn't
she just stop and rest and then come back and meet me so that she
didn't get tendonitis? But until you're faced with stopping, it's
impossible to know how hard it is. You can't just stop. However good
the excuse is, however sensible the reasoning, there's just an
overwhelming drive going on in your head that pays no attention to
anything like reason or need. It doesn't matter how many people tell
you how amazing you are, how far you've walked, how incredible
enough it has been, you can't stop. So Kris didn't want to stop. She
did want to be here, to walk. But couldn't. I wish I had been more
sympathetic, I wish I had listened more. I wish she had talked more.
I wish she had been more reasonable. Would I have been more
reasonable in her position? Who can say. It's been hard, this walking,
but not walking is really a much harder option.

Klickitat means 'beyond' in Chinook.

Ray Jardine speaks of those who find any excuse to give up,
the underlying reason, he reckons, being because they are not
getting enough food or the right kind of food.

Show me somebody who is not enjoying their hike, and I will
show you someone who is eating nutritionally deficient foods.[15]

Food is important, and much as I hate to admit it, meat seems almost essential. Nearly ever town-stop my body craves a huge slab of meat. I have met people who are eating vegetarian and doing well—the Sprouts as they became known, also without a stove, who sprouted their nuts and seeds and had incredible salads for lunch. Something known as GORP which stands for 'Good Old Raisins and Peanuts' is the staple snack food of many hikers. Now, I don't really go in for nuts and seeds, especially not mixed nuts and seeds. Accordingly, Kris packed all our nuts and seeds in separate bags which took a huge amount of time. This may sound fussy but listen to those instincts. Something inside me knew before the hike that I wasn't going to be able to stomach very many nuts and seeds over a sustained period of time. I've since learnt that most nuts actually contain certain degrees of toxins—different people have different tolerance levels. It's not a question of being able to subsist on food you don't like or don't enjoy: I loved my time in Bolivia, but food is not what you go there for. The national dish is cow's stomach lining, which has the texture of a used car-tyre, and chuños, which are freeze-dried potatoes that look like donkey turds. Long distance hiking pushes your body to its limits and it will invariably crave what you need, and reject what you don't need. Hiking in this sense is a bit like being pregnant, it can bring out all sorts of very random cravings in you.

We wanted different things and if you're going to be hiking together you have to make allowances for this. I craved beans and Mexican food and leapt in delight when I discovered dried refried beans in the Hiker Box. Kris wanted porridge oats and hated dried milk. I wanted granola and thought that juice mix was a waste of weight. Satisfy yourself. Pack separate food if necessary, separate snacks at least—I have hardly touched a nut or seed since Kris left.

I don't think this is about food, though my appetite in town would suggest I am missing sheer volume if nothing else. This is about feet. If I could carry less my feet would not take so much pressure. Perhaps I should walk fewer miles each day. But that means carrying more food. And besides, time is running out.

I could have stopped. I didn't. Two days ago I was crying as the water tumbled by Eagle Creek Falls realising my feet really could not go on. Then I got to town and met up with Vive, Glen, Turtle and Lora again. Also briefly met two girls called Kadiddle and Wonderwoman. Ate food, had a bath, slept in a motel and got emails of:

"Stop? Don't be ridiculous!" from my mother.

I'm going on for now. I'm not going to think anymore than that because I want to walk. I don't want to stop. I'm just going on for now.

In 1804 Meriwether Lewis and William Clarke set out with nearly 50 men from St. Louis, the town where the Missouri and Mississippi rivers meet. They headed upstream along the Missouri to Lemihi Pass where they joined the Colombia River and canoed down into Oregon Country. Russia, Spain, Britain and America all had 'claims' to the pleasant lands of Oregon Country (to say nothing of the indigenous people living there at the time) which ranged from Mexico (later to become California) at the 42nd parallel to the 54° 40 line (the start of the modern day border between Canada and Alaska). Russia and Spain were easily persuaded to drop any notion of such a claim and in the 1840s the chant went up in Congress 'Fifty-four forty or fight!' as regards the British claim. President Polk took up a strong stance and the British, it seems, not overly keen to fight after their previous escapades against the Americans, quickly conceded the land up to the 49th parallel. Hence this border I am walking to. Oregon was divided in two and Washington State came into being in 1889.

Day 149—2255.1 trail miles north
Road 5603

When a horse is lame on all four legs it appears sound.

When do you stop? When the voice in your head warns of being crippled for the rest of your life. I didn't even make it to lunchtime today; my feet are finally refusing to walk any further. I stopped several miles short of what I'd hoped (after 12/13 miles rather than 15/16) and plunged my feet into an icy cold pool. Every now and then ice breaks from the glacier that feeds the river and you can hear the roar as it crashes into the gorge.

Tasha, as much as this means to you, you cannot do it. You must stop. You are twenty-six-years-old. You, especially you, especially after this, will not be able to live the rest of your life happily if you cannot walk.

My feet go back into the water until the cold gets too much to bear. I am hobbling. Every step hurts. You *must* stop.

Vive turned up and we cooked our lunches, me wondering nostalgically if this would be the last time that I used my lovely little tin-can stove that Staggering Willy made me, whilst thinking automatically that it really was about time I got a wind shield.

"Vive," I say, "I'm thinking of stopping."

Vive nods.

"I'm tired too," he says.

"No, I mean really stopping. I can't walk."

We had planned to camp after some 21+ miles near Swampy Creek, but moved it forward to a '*very nice campsite*' (according to the guide book) between Muddy Fork River and Lava Spring. The decision was really to stop before the road—there was a road on the map, we weren't sure where it went as that was off the map, but it was a road.

The 'very nice campsite' was a nice enough small clearing surrounded by water. Vive strung his tarp to the tree and I pegged out the fly to my tent (I had stopped carrying the whole tent—less weight). I decided to stop. I ate two rolls and two helpings of humous for dinner. I ate all my cookie supply. There. Now you have to stop or else you will run out of food.

But still I couldn't decide. I must stop. I must stop. Sleep was not a tossing turning affair because narrow sleeping bags do not allow you to toss or turn very easily. And anyway I was trying to keep my feet raised on the small hump of my clothes to let the blood drain back out of them and reduce the swelling. But I lay deep in indecision all night, knowing that in the morning my feet would feel that bit better again and I would be able to walk two or three miles in mild discomfort only. But this was the last road. The last possible exit before the Goat Rocks Wilderness and White Pass 43 miles away. Only 43 miles. If I don't leave now, I have to make it all that way. And ultimately I will be putting Vive in danger if I keep trying. I am a liability.

So the next morning, feeling dogged and resigned, I crawled to a road, a new beautifully paved road, and waited. And waited. And waited. It wasn't even a restful wait, as the bees kept us hopping up and down. Vive kept me amused as we thought up notes to leave for Turtle and Lora knowing as they did our reputation for bickering—we now introduce ourselves as the year-before-the-divorce couple.[16]

And waited.

I thought about the forlorn entry in the post office register at Cascade Locks—Itchy or Scratchy, one of them, had '*broken her foot*'. A stress fracture? Something more serious? Did she fall coming down to Eagle Creek Falls? Or charging in leaps and bounds down a bank in an attempt to cut off a switchback? (I know, not strictly ethical, but we've all done it.) Scratchy (or Itchy) had gone on without her, having hooked up with the guy who has the adopted wolfhound. The boy from the group, now re-christened Captain America, has been running up and down every mountain the trail passes and therefore getting a bit behind. Rise and Shine had also bowed out:

"*We are not enjoying it,*" said their note. "*The weather is too bad.*"

I'm just another one of many who cannot walk the whole trail. It is beyond me.

And waited.

Vive finally offered to walk to the top of the road, where he found a sign saying '*ROAD CLOSED—Entry by permission of the Yakima Indian Reservation only*'. Ahh. So we started walking down the road in the other direction. It petered out into poor dirt roads.

It seems so odd to be essentially in the middle of nowhere (from a non-native perspective) and suddenly come across such a perfect road. Why didn't they pave the road all the way from here to the next paved road (which, it turns out, is about 13 miles away)? Why just start here?

The Yakima people are one of the few Amerindian groups that survived the holocaust of civilisation. They still fish on the Columbia River, after winning back their fishing rights following a series of 'fish-ins' in the 1960s. Back in 1855 the Yakimas along with the Nez Perces and Umatillas ('water rippling over sand') and others were called to sign a treaty in Walla Walla. The Amerindians arrived on horseback at full gallop, their faces painted with white, red and yellow, their bodies decked in full warrior dress, yelling their war cry. The treaties were signed, much to the disgust of Chief Kamiakim of the Yakimas, guaranteeing the Amerindians the usual reservations, schools and economic help in exchange for land. The governor of Washington told Chief Kamiakim they would not have to move for a while yet—two or three years. Within twelve days he had opened the area to settlement and the Anglo-Americans were flocking west in the name of manifest destiny. Unfortunately for the Nez Perces, gold was discovered at the heart of their reservation in Wallowa Valley and, despite heroic resistance and presidential decree, they were bullied and hounded out. In 1877 the state troops came to round up those who not only refused to be moved, but dared to fight for their land. Hin-mah-too-yah-lat-kekht led his people on a 1700 mile journey—the length of the PCT through California—to Canada, fighting and escaping from the army at their heels. They were forced to surrender, tired and cold, with the children freezing to death, just 30 miles from the border. Hin-mah-too-yah-lat-kekht was never allowed to return to his land.

And I'm stopping because my feet hurt. Obviously, in my case, lack of necessity is the key thing—there's a small voice at the back of my head which occasionally mutters, "Um, are you not meant to be enjoying yourself?" And I am, have been. I won't remember the pain (though my feet might well at this rate), but will no doubt look back on the trip with nostalgia and lupin-tinted glasses. So the sound of an engine was both blissful and sad. Am I leaving the trail? I can't do this. But common sense says stop, before you do any permanent damage. Though maybe it's too late for that already. The engine was a jeep driven by George from the Reservation who picked us up on his way huckleberry picking and drove us into town, where I managed to see a doctor.

The doctor asked, "Are your feet normally this colour?"

Does anybody have feet normally this colour?

1000 miles ago my arches were collapsing. They ached and twinged and sometimes at night had small spasms of their own volition. But generally after about five to ten minutes of walking, when they had become more flexible, they forgot themselves. I could walk quite happily until the afternoon at least. The insoles I bought really did help to remedy this problem and I have walked much better with them. They are, however, designed for ski-boots and skiers, not for walkers and so are rigid, hard plastic structures. Now my feet are purple with bruising and the soles are swollen. My middle toes have gone numb except for one which tingles continuously. And it does not improve with walking, it gets steadily worse and worse and more and more painful.

The Jardine in me says, "Buy trainers! NOW!"

It's not money—what's being a bit more overdrawn when you've the chance of fulfilling a dream? I just really don't know whether they would be better or not. They would definitely be more comfortable on the soles of my feet, they would help with the bruising. But I am so near the end, to start all over again with blisters, is that really necessary? And just when we're getting into the bad weather. Wet feet can equal hypothermia and I find it difficult to keep my feet warm at the best of times. How I long for my plastic shoes (lost somewhere back in the Sierras—I now cross rivers wearing hiking socks which is exceptionally painful with my feet being in the state that they are) to wear just as a change of shoe.

The doctor said to rest for at least six days. I stopped for two, which seemed a good compromise and rested in Packwood at the old wooden Packwood Hotel which was not only the best in town but also the cheapest and had a piano. Vive came too. Which was nice of him.

We are an odd pair. I am not convinced that he really likes me. Nor am I convinced that I really like him. We bicker and bug and pick and yet when he has gone I miss his presence. When he is not out of humour he is great company—Vive knows how to 'spin a yarn' as they say and is a fantastic story-teller. His normal theme is himself, his own exploits, and his life, but he does it in such a style that the stories are hilarious.

Packwood does not abound with shoe shops. In fact there are none. So the whole ponder above turned out to be a non-starter in any event. I sit on the wooden veranda of this small rectangular house that looks a bit like someone lowered it from the sky, rolling my feet on Coca-Cola cans—turns out the drink does have some uses after all . . . .

Day 152—2256.9 trail miles north
White Pass

Onwards. Onwards and upwards (in a map-reading kind of way, though the general trend from the Columbia River to Canada is also up). Set off from White Pass, heading for Snoqualmie Pass. The first night out, we camped by a beautiful lake, and were awoken by some strange noises. A woman screaming was my first thought. Or scraping metal. None the wiser, we set off the next morning. Then close to me, in the forest, just a few hundred feet away, a screech that sounded like a cross between a donkey and an elephant. What is this?

We later met three happy hunters who fed us beef jerky and gave us a demonstration of their bugle. It is, it turns out, elk rutting season and the elks scream out challenges. The hunters use their bugles to attract challenging males into shooting distance. These hunters, thankfully, were way too merry to keep quiet enough or aim straight enough to hit an elk. A hiker on the other hand . . . .

Day 154—2327.5 trail miles north
Snoqualmie Pass

Walk through three days of clear-cuts in the rain or hitch? Once you've started, you can't stop.

So I'm no longer going to walk every single step of the trail in one thru-hike. I don't think it matters too much. I'm injured, I need the rest. But I'm in Washington, close to the end; I've walked far enough to stop worrying about each individual mile. Do you remember Beaker, the hiker with the sprained ankle on the first day? We met Beaker again a few days ago, walking southbound. He stayed put by Hauser Creek until he could hobble enough to do the remaining six miles to Lake Morena. Then he rested there, then each day he did a little more until he had built his strength up to walk properly. You have to admire his determination, not to be thwarted on the first day. Kris walked 650 miles and could have stopped on Day Four. She wanted to do as Beaker did, walk a little each day until her ankle was better. We did stop and rest, we did slow down, but a combination of my will and our worry about crossing the Mojave any later than we did (middle of June) meant we had to do at least 15 miles a day. I could not have walked 30 miles a day consistently to make up time, nor could I have carried enough water to go from source to source—any later than we came and the majority of creeks dry up and the caches are found empty. I don't think Kris could have done either. Unfortunately for Kris she was as determined as Beaker, more determined than me. There are other hikers I've met who've skipped every mile possible (some even with great pride!) or missed out large chunks. Beaker is a strong experienced hiker and knew what he was capable of. Apparently he was just a day behind me all through Northern California when I thought I was the last thru-hiker. On reaching Castella he decided his chances of reaching Canada before the bad weather were slight and so headed north on a bus to hike south from the border. This makes me even more convinced not to walk these missing miles—the weather is deteriorating, the time getting shorter, better to miss miles now rather than get stuck in a snowstorm far from anywhere, by myself, with my feet too sore to move. And the north of Washington is very remote.

All this obviously makes good sense. Though I still feel I'm telling myself to justify missing miles of ugly clear-cuts in the rain. Stupid.

In the pouring rain we came down to Chinook Pass, passing a family that reminded me a little of my own, determined to walk in spite of the weather, and got a series of rides the rest of the way to Snoqualmie, driving past the ugly square blocks of missing forest. I see these bald patches with curiosity. This is what people have been talking about for miles, the ugly clear-cuts of Oregon country. There are patches dotted across the views, patches of missing trees. Blisterfree, a hiker I met near Castella, didn't want to see it.

"On the AT you have a mile either side of aesthetic bordering, it's much better. You get the illusion at least of wilderness."

I would prefer to see it all though. This hike isn't about seeing an illusion. It's not about living an illusion. This is about walking a dream and I want to see everything as it is from the desert-like landscape around Los Angeles to the scars of roads slicing up the country, to the missing grizzlies . . . .

Is Britain beautiful? I tell them yes. Scotland I say is beyond words and think nostalgically of the rolling sheep-nibbled hills and raging sea. And England with its patchwork of green fields. The trees have been gone so long that they are the patches in our landscape.

Walking through old forest growth is a magical experience. The floor of such a forest is a graveyard of dead and rotting branches all covered by a damp green moss. The trees themselves rise up so far that their trunks are all unhuggable (not that I've taken to hugging trees—honest). It is never sunny in such a forest and it is always silent.

In Snoqualmie we met up with Glen who had already called the Bed and Breakfast for hikers. Bob, the owner, showed up to take us there.

"No hurry," says Bob. "Let's go for a drink."

We picked up our re-supply boxes and met in the bar where

Bob offered us drinks on him. None of us particularly wanted a drink, but Bob was insistent. I went up to the bar where the bar lady rejected my ID (my passport!) on the grounds that the date of birth had been hand-written rather than typed. I asked her if she would have me phone the British government to complain. Eventually she accepted my visa as proof and I ordered two drinks to go on the tab.

"There is no tab," she said.

I looked round and Bob had disappeared. I paid for the drinks. We sat down and took a sip. Bob came back. Then a woman stormed in and announced to the entire bar:

"YOU SAID you would be FIVE MINUTES, DINNER'S been on the TABLE!!!!!"

All heads turned.

"We were just having a drink," stuttered Bob.

"DON'T MAKE ME MAKE A SCENE . . ." she threatened.

They left. Bob re-entered immediately and said we had to go. Unwanted, undrunk drinks stayed on the table, and Bob drove us to the B & B.

It rained all night and all the next day. We asked the B & B to take us back up to the Pass—the ride was included in the deal we had made.

"You're free to walk," said the woman.

Bob was shut away in the kitchen and was not allowed to come out. So we left the B & B and went to the hotel instead, hoping other hikers would arrive to help get the price down.

And, one by one, the hikers came in. First two women, Kadiddle and Wonderwoman, who had left the day before, walked eight miles, camped and got so wet they decided to do what no thru-hiker ever does—turn around and walk back, soaked to the skin. Then the Menacing Vegetables crawled in, now heading southbound having flip-flopped (after California they travelled up to Canada and were hiking Washington and Oregon in reverse). For them this is the final straw, their hike is over. Horror stories emerge of sleeping in three inches of water, the trail a stream, minor step-over creeks now raging torrents difficult to ford. Pickle's sleeping bag was so wet it weighed more than my pack. Drenched. We share, six to a room, and dry off in the sauna. On the TV there are flood warnings for, of all places, Snoqualmie.

Winter is definitely on the way.

THE RESCUE

Day 158—2396.6 trail miles north
Snoqualmie Pass

The next day six of us hiked out together: Kadiddle, Wonder, Vive, Glen, Wonderwoman and myself. Wonderwoman, or Sarah from Switzerland, started at the beginning of June from the Canadian border. The snow was still thick and heavy, at least ten foot deep, and there was no trail as such. Using her compass, maps, crampons and two ice-axes she crawled along the steep-sided mountains at a pace of ten miles a day, watching the avalanches fall around her. As soon as she hit the first road she escaped to civilisation and went south to Mexico to start again from there on 12th June. Since then she has walked 30 miles a day with a 70-pound pack, even through the desert with no water caches when many of the creeks were dry. Hence the trail name Wonderwoman. She is a professional athlete who specialises in extreme sports (like jumping out of helicopters to snowboard down mountains). Kadiddle, who I met at the send-off, is, like me, hiking for charity. She is raising money and awareness for Project Steam, an after-school programme for kids at risk (www.steamteam.org). Wonder is a Buddhist from Oregon who knows the trail well, having walked Oregon and Washington previously.

We walked and climbed through the beautiful Alpine Lakes Wilderness, the weather clearing just enough to see the steep-sided valleys with their wash of red and yellow huckleberry bushes.

'This airy section is often dry,' says the guide book. Not now it's not. Step-over creeks have turned into big boulder-hops, and boulder-hops into fords. There is water everywhere, pouring off the sides of the mountains, making for spectacular waterfalls.

Two days out and I'm sitting by one such waterfall looking at the map. I see a shortcut. We debate—no-one has a problem cutting off miles at this stage, but our maps are ten years old, the trail could be unmaintained, and then there are all these creeks to consider. We decide to give it a go. Half a mile down this trail, we come across Tom. Tom is asking for food. He has run out, he says. Tom is wet. And hypothermic. Hypothermia has to be one of the biggest killers in the mountains and it can take hold frighteningly fast. Gradually the story emerges: he isn't properly equipped, fell into a creek, has no dry clothes.

We each slip into rescue role. Vive makes hot chocolate and he, Wonder and Kadiddle get Tom out of his wet clothes. Sarah and Glen unpack their packs and repack emergency kit only. I work out a route to town and the trails they need to follow. It is 31 miles to Highway 2 and a nine-mile hitch to Skykomish from there. Snoqualmie is closer, but there is a 5000-foot climb and the terrain is rough. There is a ranger station about six to seven miles to the east but most likely it will be unmanned as summer is over. The ranger station is serviced by a dirt road but it disappears off the end of the map to we don't know where. I tell Sarah and Glen the options.

"I not go back to Snoquolmie," says Sarah her eyes rolling. "Already two times I have been along this piece of trail. I not going three times, and not up this hill."

We decide the best option is for them to go on to Highway 2. The ranger station is too much of a risk as it might be many miles before it hits a main road.

Vive feeds the two hot chocolate as well as Tom and we give them all our chocolate bars. They set off for a 31-mile run, having already walked ten miles in the morning. It is 12.30 p.m.

Tom, an elderly man, had left Snoqualmie ten days ago. The weather turned extremely nasty and he decided to turn back, abandoning his wet sleeping bag. He managed about five miles and camped. The next day he had to cross the now very ferocious Lemah Creek. There was a log, but he slipped and fell into the creek.

The point of rendezvous has been chosen as Pete Lake, which is back across the Creek. We hope there is enough clearance for a helicopter there (we are presently in thick forest). Kadiddle and I leave with our packs and attempt to cross. The log is extremely wet and slippery and the water deep on either side. We turn back. There is another log crossing upstream which has branches sticking up. It, too, proves impassable with a pack. We are perhaps being slightly more cautious than usual, but this is the creek into which Tom has just fallen and also Glen has been filling us with horror stories.

Feeling rather pleased with himself one afternoon a few months ago, Glen was ambling at a good pace along the Continental Divide Trail. He arrived at a rather notoriously deep ford in Wyoming. Another hiker had told him of a boulder hop further upstream so he set off pushing through the trees. Eventually he arrived at the spot. The river at this stage was a gorge, and some 50 feet below him, but the walls were big granite blocks. It was a jump of about a metre across and down to the opposite bank. He took his pack off, tied some string round it and threw it to the other side. It landed with a healthy plonk, not great for the camera, but hopefully it was far enough inside to be protected. So far so good. Then, just as he was getting ready to make the leap himself, his pack began to slip, ever so slowly down the rock. He watched in slow motion horror as his pack, his trail 'home' if you like, his entire survival kit, toppled into the water, taking the string with it before he could get a good hold. There was a moment of nothing as he looked down aghast into the water, and then up it bobbed and set off downstream at a healthy lick. Glen, perhaps feeling less like a romantic action hero than he would have liked, ran and leapt and crashed his way back down stream. Every few moments he would reach the edge, look down into the gorge and see his pack, further downstream than before, and sinking further and further under as it became water-logged. Eventually he arrived at a scree slope, stormed down the bank, plunged into the river, and managed to rescue the pack. The moment of relief passed quickly as he realised that it was now getting dark (and therefore cold) and every piece of warm clothing/tent/sleeping bag he owned was wet. Luckily for Glen he had a lighter. He got a fire going, dried some things out, and stayed warm.

Kadiddle and I look at the logs, she perhaps would give it a go. It's worth quite a lot to have dry feet when hiking, especially in

Washington. How I wish I'd paid more attention to the PCT guru, good old Ray Jardine. He preached serious pre-hike training, not only preparing for the walking (carrying more and more weight each time), and the food/cooking (so you know what you can stomach), but also practising one's 'circus' skills—balancing on one leg in order to cross logs like this one whilst juggling heavy and bulky objects.

It's true my thigh muscles are now big and strong, and my sense of balance must have improved along with all that. Some of the female Menacing Vegetables had even mastered the art of peeing with their packs on whilst standing up. Definitely beyond me. But is this? The smooth tree trunk glistens as the water sprays over it. The ford is three times as wide as the tree trunk. For a fleeting moment I'm 13 years old, a fantastic 'dirty dancer', and Patrick Swayze is beckoning me on to the log whilst standing on one leg. The moment passes; balancing has never been one of my specialities—the next image is of the true-life thirteen-year-old falling rather painfully (and very embarrassingly) off the bar during the school Gym Display.

"Let's ford," I say.

As fords go it is very wide and painful on the feet, cold but fairly shallow. Kadiddle, with her sandals and trekking poles strides quickly across. Wearing my spare hiking socks and longing again for my lovely plastic shoes and the poles I started with, I struggle over, my pack loosened at the waist. Each step is painful, awkward and unsteady. The deepest ford so far was Evolution Creek in Yosemite. In Yosemite more than ten hikers drown each year. Probably the most dangerous crossing on the trip so far for me was Milky Creek in the Mount Jefferson Wilderness.

Mount Jefferson

White from glacier deposits, Milky Creek rises daily and the guide book warns you to cross before 11 in the morning. It is so cold that from the minute you step in you lose all feeling in your feet. It is a good raging torrent by the afternoon—the time at which I crossed. I spent a good deal of time and effort clambering half a mile or so upstream looking for a boulder hop, but to no avail. Although the scare factor was considerably less higher up (the trail crosses just above the gorge and if you did slip, well, let's just say it's a long way down), the water was considerably more ferocious. Just as I was giving up, Steve and Celest arrived on the scene, and the three of us crossed together.

A mile on from crossing Lemah Creek we arrive at Pete Lake and I leave Kadiddle to set up camp and go back to pick up Glen and Sarah's gear, taking the long way round via the bridges further upstream. A mile back and I meet Wonder and Vive who are trying to walk Tom back to Pete Lake, this time missing out the ford. Tom does not want to go back, nor does he walk fast but we all eventually get to Pete

Lake. We persuade Tom to stay the night in front of the fire. My
sleeping bag is donated to Tom for the night and Kadiddle and I
share hers—luckily it wasn't snowing like the night before.

Now it is beautifully sunny and the lake is glistening. Tom's
clothes are drying. We cook hot chocolate and soup for him and
gently talk him out of leaving. It is midday the next day and no
rescue has come as yet. We are saving our fuel, so time to get the
fire going again for lunch.

So near the end. So close.

Sarah and Glen hiked fast with light packs but over tough terrain.
After several difficult creek crossings and a struggle up to Cathedral
Pass they eventually stopped at 10 p.m. after 21 miles. The next
morning they had to wait for their shoes to thaw out and arrived at
the road at 2.30 p.m. There were some construction workers there
and they called 911 immediately. And then nothing happened. A
state trooper showed up, asked them some questions, and left. They
were starving hungry. Then a deputy showed up, asked the same
questions, took them to Burger King and then to Snoqualmie. Sarah
and Glen had walked out into a different county to the one we were
waiting in and an argument had begun as to who was to rescue us.
Sarah, who truly deserves her trail name Wonderwoman, set to work
in a passionate stream of thick French-accented English and astonished
the sheriff's department into submission.

If anyone can make things happen then it is Wonderwoman.
She told us that as she entered the wilderness just after Walker Pass
she signed the register as we all had done a month or so earlier.
Several days later she was approaching Monache Meadows and
noticed a forest fire on the horizon. Then she saw a helicopter and
thought 'Oh, good, they are dealing with it.' The helicopter,
however, was circling mysteriously round and round as if looking
for someone, and when they spotted Sarah, a fire-fighter was lowered
down in front of her.

"Excuse me Ma'am, are you Sarah M____?" asked the fire-
fighter.

Wonderwoman confirmed that she was.

"Well my captain has ordered me to pick you up, Ma'am."

WALKING DOWN A DREAM

"You want me, to go with you? In the helicopter?" asked the French voice.

"Yes Ma'am."

"I have not time for this; I walking to Canada."

He finally convinced her that he would get in big trouble if she didn't go and, as bait, suggested it would be fun to ride in a helicopter.

"This, I do everyday," said Sarah. "Only in my work, we jump out of it, without the rope."

Must have been the best knock-back a fire-fighter's ever had. Having been delivered safely to the base in Kernville, Wonderwoman demanded to see the captain and demanded that he fly her back in to the same spot where she had just been picked up from, fire permitting. He laughed. Then said it was dangerous.

"More dangerous than sleeping here, with 200 fire-fighters?" retorted Sarah.

Twenty minutes later he had agreed to take her back the next day, at the expense of the fire-service.

Back at the lake we had given up hope for the day and were cooking Tom's evening soup on a roaring fire. And then came the sound of the helicopter blades. We ran back and forth, waving our silver Mylar blankets to show them where we were and then to put the fire out, as the wind from the helicopter sent everything flying. They managed to land in a small space of brush and the sheriff (from the other county) came running out, splashing through the water like Sylvester Stallone in a Hollywood movie.

"Sir? I'm here to take you out, sir!" he roared at Tom who, somewhat disturbed, responded with a firm

"No!"

It took us 40 minutes to persuade him to leave in the helicopter after the sheriff's gung-ho attitude. By this time it was dark. We sat around what had been the campfire for a bit longer but then went to bed.

12.30 a.m.—"Bears in the camp!!"

Startled, we fumbled around for our lights, bears?

"Bears!" said Glen's voice.

Bears? Turned out to be 'beers' in a Tennessee accent, and it was Sarah and Glen waking us up. They had hiked back in (via the ranger station) with the other county's rescue team. We packed up and all hiked out to the waiting jeeps and then to Snoqualmie where the sheriff of King County arranged for us to stay for free.

Sarah's sheriff called us back outside just as we were about to stumble into the beds.

"What?" demanded six bleary-eyed hikers.

He pointed upwards. As if to herald our safe arrival, a strange green drift of light wandered across the sky. At first it was an ever-expanding beam, then it broke into small clusters of brightness. Then it was a slow, unpredictable dance of mass, like a giant lava lamp at work. The Northern Lights. Snoqualmie is named, I'm told, after another light, the moon (in the language of the Snoqualmie people).

5.30 a.m.—sleep.

Now, we are a group, firmly fixed together: 'Wonderwoman and The Wolf Pack'.

The Wolfpack minus Vive

CANADA

Day 159—2477.1 trail miles north
Lake Valhalla

Thomas R. Lovejoy of Cascade Locks, who, according to his sign, conducts 'Marriages, Construction and Auto-sales', told me, "You're putting 30 years on, you know, doing this. You'll be a cripple by 40."

The rest has definitely given my feet a little leeway. But in case anyone has any misconceptions about thru-hiking, it doesn't make you feel fit and strong. It takes at least three weeks for the blisters to go. Then you have a month or so of really feeling good leg-wise but your back never stops complaining of its load. And then any number of body parts begin to collapse. Usually it starts with the feet—many thru-hikers lose toenails, or (like me) lose all feeling in their toes apart from a vague numb awareness that they are there. Then the arches begin to collapse or the ankles are strained. Then the knees ache or the pelvis gets out of place. And the back carries on moaning the whole way. Four months into the hike you stop feeling good and start feeling tired. Standing up first thing in the morning is crippling. Balancing or standing on one foot is virtually impossible. And everyday you get more tired.

Wonder (or Buddha Wolf, his other name) chants the new 'hiking mantra' as he walks along:

"My name is Wonder. I love hiking. I am happy."

He disappears off to chant at various times in the day, as well as from his tent early in the morning. I have no idea what he is asking for or giving thanks to, but the rhythm, the steadiness of the murmur fits so well into this serene landscape, it hardly seems to matter. Waking gently to this low sound at 4.30 a.m. beside the apparition of an almost see-through mountain, I imagine an ancient people praying to the apu (mountain god) simply for their 'wonder'.

"Vonderrr?" sings Sarah, rolling the last 'r', "Vonderrr, where are you? We go now."

I join in with Wonder's daytime chant.

"My name is Natasha. I love hiking. I am happy."

My body has taken a pounding. But then there are the occasional blips when the urge to storm uphill comes back and I get some satisfaction climbing up one of the many switchbacks in the Glacier Peak Wilderness. After some magnificent ridge-walking we scrambled to the top of Portal Peak for a 360-degree panorama of the North Cascades. We stood on top of a rock, raised our hands and voices skywards and howled across the valleys. The mountain air gives you a wash of euphoria. In front of us looms the almighty chunk of Glacier Peak (10,501 feet), away in the distance to the south is the ghostly white dome of Rainier (14,410 feet), and there, on the Canadian border, almost within touching distance is Mount Baker (10,778 feet). I am so happy to be here.

A truly inspiring moment.

Vive has not been feeling well—blacking out and falling over which makes us all a bit perturbed. Hikers have a responsibility not just to themselves but others. It's all very well and nice and romantic to set off solo into the mountains without a care, but if something does go wrong, you can put the people who find you at risk as well as yourself. And one should think not least of the King County Search and Rescue Crew (and tax payers) who more often than not pick up bodies each week. Sarah decided to take Vive off down the mountain towards a trailhead where he can hitch into town and see a doctor, and then climb back up again to catch us up. I can't quite believe how strong this woman is. We are camped on a pass and the sun is setting around us. The scenery is magnificent and we howl our way around the mountains. Glen and Wonder run off to climb every possible peak. Large furry hoary marmots pop up from their burrows surrounded by the golden-red dying huckleberry bushes and eye us suspiciously. I am tired and my body aches but I am also happy. How good to finish like this.

I had heard about Kadiddle before I met her. Hikers spoke in awe of the woman who managed to get a free bed at every stop, free meals with mountain rangers, and rides to wherever she wanted to go. It was all a bit puzzling.

Charm is not the right word. She radiates goodwill like a pre-commercialised Christmas carol. Not just goodwill, good free will; with Kadiddle anything is possible. It's not a challenge to prove oneself, just a quiet confidence boost. She urges everyone to live their dreams.

Now I've made her sound like a Christian hippie who might suddenly burst into a rendition of Amazing Grace round the campfire or a new-age theraputerised American who might give classes packed with clichés and cheese, and she's really not like that at all. She's a happy harmony of New York Jewish/Italian with a level head and a great flair for not only dreaming, but actually doing, the impossible. Why is it so easy to describe irritations and so hard to portray goodness?

I have nothing planned for when I get back. No project, no dream, no goal. A career, a job—what will I end up doing? I think it might be time to stop wandering aimlessly around. I definitely don't need to do any more soul-searching, or challenge myself to fulfil the sublime and the ridiculous. I think I might even want to have children at some stage. What am I saying?

2.4 kids, life in suburbia, nine-to-five job and the pub on Friday night? And what has happened in this six months? What cultural references will I not understand? Is the talk all of *Survivor*? Or the thirty odd people who have been living on an island off Scotland for the year—the *Castaway* crew—watched by television cameras? *Big Brother*? Reality TV and invasion of privacy? Peace and isolation performed to a few million. People (people I know, people I have met briefly on the trail, people from the Internet who I have never met) write and tell me they are proud of me. That I am amazing. I don't feel amazing. I feel like I have survived.

There are two roads through the forest: one includes friends, contentment and a feeling of having sold out; the other loneliness, fulfilment and images of becoming one of those people who talk too much and can't listen because they are so delighted to see another human being. The latter is definitely 'the one less travelled', but the romantic always ends up costing you more.

There's a bit in *Gone With the Wind* where Scarlet realises that no-one really likes her, and someone says something along the lines of, "Never mind dear, you'll make a wonderful grandmother."

Maybe I'll make a good grandmother. Or mad auntie with fantastical stories and exotic presents.

A brief stop in Stehekin where we met up again with a healthier Vive, who, typically, has had quite a few adventures of his own and is eager to tell us one of his 'tall' stories. There is a road *in* Stehekin, one road, but there is no road *to* Stehekin. You can walk in, or you can come by boat across Lake Chelan. It's very inaccessible. We had left Vive on the wrong side of the mountain so to speak and there are only two road passes—Stevens Pass, by Skykomish, and Rainy Pass. Vive walked out to a road and managed to get a lift to the main road and a gas station. There he spent six hours waiting for a ride. Eventually a 30-something blond-haired woman turned up.—There are cries of "in your dreams."

"No!" protests Vive. "No really she was really quite good looking, I mean not that I was thinking that way or anything, but she was pretty."

"Yeah, yeah, yeah."

"Do you want to hear this story or don't you?"—

The woman, Georgie, went into the gas station and bought a loaf of bread and a tin of tuna. Vive followed her in and asked for a lift. After a bit of negotiation and a payment of 20 dollars—

"You paid her!"

"She needed the money ok!"

"You paid her . . . I can't believe you paid her!"

"The Babe in action . . . ."

"If you don't want to hear . . . ."—

Georgie agreed to take Vive over Rainy Pass to the next town of

Winthrop where he could get a lift to Chelan (he hoped). Vive clambered into the car and watched Georgie pick up a screw driver from the dashboard which she used to start the engine. They got talking; Vive always 'gets talking'. Georgie it turned out, was homeless, and had been living in the woods for the last two years. She and a small group lived off the land—deer, rodents and berries, a diet supplemented by the odd supply of tuna. Vive persuaded her to take him all the way to Chelan for an extra 20 dollars. From there he would have to get the five-hour ferry ride to Stehekin. Rainy Pass is a steep pass and Georgie's car chugged slowly all the way up, finally collapsing just before the brow of the hill. Disaster. There was little to be done, so Georgie shrugged her shoulders and they both got out of the car to hitch. Within ten minutes Vive was relieved to hear another car climbing the hill and it rolled off the road just a hundred yards short of them. He hurried over only to find the driver cursing and kicking the wheels; the hill had proved too much for that car as well. A third car arrived on the scene within an hour and managed to make it over the top. Vive said goodbye to Georgie and got a lift to Chelan. Now Vive had managed to leave his wallet and credit cars somewhere at the last stop. His cash total had been 50 dollars, which left him in Chelan in the dark with ten dollars. He wandered from hotel to motel and eventually found somewhere that would let his sister pay by credit card over the phone. The next day he saw a doctor who told him he had had a virus and gave him something to take and then he successfully caught the ferry to Stehekin.

The Wolfpack meanwhile were gorging in the best food-stop on the whole trek, an incredible German bakery with fresh loaves and cakes that you can only dream about.

Then the last leg. The weather couldn't have been better—cold, crisp and clear. The views are incredible. The snow is light, dry and crunchy.

We sit around the campfire each night (Wolf Dream, Singing Wolf, Buddha Wolf, Running Wolf, and Talking Wolf—Wonderwoman has departed, as she walked this section back in June) and talk. Where were you five, ten, twenty years ago?

"Doing my first stand-up comedy."

"Directing a play."

"Cooking for a crew of builders."

"Working on a fishing boat in Alaska."

"Involved in a potato chip riot in high school." (?!)

Where will you be ten years from now?

"Don't know."

"On the ocean."

"Cooking vegan food."

"Published."

"Living my dreams."

We are all living our dreams. Can we continue? Kadiddle and I have started planning the next dream. It doesn't involve walking. Anywhere.

We reach what we call 'our border', the aesthetic border of Lakeview Ridge. We stay on the top in the cold and watch the sun setting over the huge lump of Mount Baker and then descend to camp our last night by a lake.

Lakeview Ridge

Kadiddle will not camp close to any trees that are leaning or old or creaking. I think at first that the likelihood of being hit by a falling tree is fairly remote. However, she soon tells me that I'm wrong. Her first week out on the Appalachian Trail, Kadiddle was in a tent with another girl during a storm. They heard the crack and the tree fell on to their tent, straight between the two sleeping bodies. Even more fortunately there was a rock just in front of the tent and it took the bulk of the weight. The girl she was with escaped unhurt; Kadiddle suffered crushed knees. She rested, immobile for ten days, and then reloaded her pack and went on to complete the AT that year.

Kadiddle and I are alone—the others have chosen to have their own space on the last night. Kadiddle puts the tent up and I build a fire in the ever-darkening dusk. We huddle around it and unscrew our half bottles of cheap red wine that we have carried in for the occasion. The fire can't compete with the silent cold and the wine is not whisky. It's dark, the forest is near and the comfort of the open lake too far. Night time is wilderness time. Then begins the slightest softness that it is possible to hear—snow gently falling. In a minute the ground is white, in a few minutes it is crunchy. We kick the fire out and retreat to our sleeping bags. I am grateful for Wonderwoman's serious weather tent and the warmth of Kadiddle beside me. Winter has arrived.

I am awoken by a scuffling near my head.

"Kadiddle," I whisper.

"What?"

"Listen."

There is a silence.

"What?" She asks louder and something growls from outside the tent.

We stay awake, listening. A bear? Some kind of coon? A cat?

"What shall we do?" asks Kadiddle.

"Make a lot of noise," say I.

We look at each other, open our mouths and both howl as loudly as we can.

"Ouw! Ouw! Oooouuuuwww!"

The animal goes.

The next morning we pack up in the cold and walk to cross

the official border at 9.45 a.m., 16th October 2000. There is a swathe cut in the forest and a monument. The group is there and we all yell and whoop and take endless photos. And then there is the small matter of an eight-mile hike out to the nearest road in Manning Park, British Columbia, Canada.

The walking is over. Mexico to Canada.

Monument

AFTER

AFTERMATH

Day 170—2658.7 trail miles north
Manning Park

Western thought is based on journeys. Traditionally perhaps, the journey was primarily religious—we fell from grace and are struggling to get back to paradise. Then there was evolution—from ape to stone age, to enlightenment, and the modern age. For many of my contemporaries it's a journey of eclectic consumerism—from that first teenage purchase of a walkman to cars, houses, DVD players and microwaves. Now there is an array of journeys available; the choice is yours—religion, love, information, identity, a mortgage, walking from Mexico to Canada. Whatever the choice, we are constantly under the illusion that we are going somewhere, the grass is greener, there is a better place waiting for us; we must progress! Our journeys are ones of self-improvement, of learning, of growing, of gaining; they are greedy all-consuming journeys with no consideration for anything or anyone who stands in the way, and there's only ever one way.

We do not appreciate the journey we have chosen. James Wilson writes that for many of the Amerindians, almost beyond our conception, life is not a journey as such. They are (were) here. Here. This is (was) Eden, the Elysium fields. How much more sense it makes to look after the earth when you think of it as your final destination. When you believe that your environment is sacred, the trees cannot be cut indefinitely, the animals cannot be eaten without thought, men cannot be killed needlessly. There was no waste in such a world, there was balance and toleration and man believed he was here to keep the balance.

Us, on the other hand, who cares when we're so assured there's always somewhere better, somewhere else?

I'm not religious. But this heaven of ours, what if it is as illusive as Atlantis, what if it is as disappointing as El Dorado? Just another level on a Scottish hill when you arrive at the top only to find there's yet another hummock above you? Onwards and upwards. There doesn't have to be a destination anymore. Life isn't bad enough. Not for me, not for most westerners. Those economic migrants leaving their hungry families in environments that would satisfy the most demanding 18-year-olds' appetite for adventure, they need destinations. We, with our comforts and happiness and satisfaction, we can afford to relish the journey, to take the time. We don't need heaven. If we just stopped and appreciated what is around us, heaven could so easily be here, be now. There are so many people out there who have the opportunity to be happy. It's never been so possible, it's up to you to take it.

It feels at first like just another town-stop—stuff yourself silly with food and look for a ride to buy more food. Only this time I phone home to say, "I'm in Canada!"

It doesn't feel real.

I'm here finally and I don't want to be. I don't want it to stop. The last few days we have cut our miles somewhat. Tired? Sore? Yes, but I think we've been spinning it out, taking our time. A month ago I couldn't wait to finish, I was done, enough, no more. Now I come to the end and I've no wish to see Vancouver. I want to walk tomorrow.

We send Vive off to look for a lift for all of us, almost as a joke. He comes back 20 minutes later and says, "I've found a ride, she'll take us anywhere." We stare in disbelief and then run to the car in case this mystery woman changes her mind. She seems very relaxed and confident, throws Vive the keys to the people-carrier and says she's just off to buy a drink. We climb in, slightly dazed. Vive bags the front. So this is 'The Babe' in action. The highway is a big one, cars and traffic. Vancouver is a big city. Numbed we stare out of the window whilst Vive gives directions and helps himself to a drink. Treat 'em mean, keep 'em keen? Kadiddle almost slaps him for being so presumptuous to this great lady. We are all a bit confused and disorientated.

We eat more and go out dancing. In hiker clothes. There's a moment of surrealism in the toilets when two girls in short black numbers and heels get the shock of their lives whilst replenishing their make up—I inadvertently reveal my seriously hairy armpits. Kadiddle complains about Vive and I explain that it's a Canadian thing, they are very direct here.

"Not *that* direct," says Kadiddle.

The lady turns out to be Vive's ex-wife who just turned up on the off-chance.

"How did you know he was coming in?" we ask.

"It was meant to be," she says.

Vive doesn't look all that convinced, but hey, it got us a lift here.

"Are there discounts for people who walked here from Mexico?" we ask everywhere.

One hotel manager explodes with laughter. No, really, we walked here. It doesn't seem real. And by the next day I miss it already. The peace, the quiet and, most of all, the fresh air. I buy clothes in the thrift shop—a bright seventies skirt and three inch platform shoes. We eat fruit by the ton and gorge in different restaurants each night. Everyone disappears one by one, back to some other non-hiking life. Kris doesn't want to see me. I catch the plane home.

December 2000
England, UK

It seems to rain every day here. I don't think I have ever seen so much rain. There are flood warnings on the rivers and the news is full of pictures of people being rescued from the windows of upper storeys and ferried down the street in boats. Britain is water-logged.

I went for a walk (just a few tame miles) and met a hiker walking from Land's End to John O'Groats. Felt absurdly 'trail-sick'. But it would be a very different thing hiking here. You couldn't do the Jardine way. Even full leather boots find it tough going in knee-deep mud and slurry puddles. But then there are pubs with roaring fires to dry off in.

I haven't found a boyfriend who's into football. Or a nine-to-five job yet either. London is heaving with people and no-one says hello to anyone else. My feet still twinge at the end of the day. I cycle and swim to try to stay fit, but that great feeling of strength has gone. Onwards and upwards? There's an awful lot to be said for the simple life in the open air. Though running water is very nice indeed, hot running water.

> *. . . we hoped some readers would walk the whole trail in one long season. Some did and some more certainly will. However, for several reasons, we no longer recommend it . . . the human body was not meant to carry heavy packs continuously over a rugged 2600-mile distance and some hikers attempting this feat developed serious bone and ligament problems in their feet and legs.*
>
> Schaffer et al, *The Pacific Crest Trail Guide Book*

Why am I only just reading this now?

So I'm back at home. I've walked 2500 miles through the wilderness, raised £12,000 for sustainability projects in Bolivia, and lost a friend.

Kris doesn't write. She sends a note every now and then, to tell me she's sold the pocketmail or that we need to update the website with new information. She can't hike anymore and is still seeing physiotherapists and podiatrists. Was it the wrong shoes, the lack of support? Or was her body just not built for it? I know that I wasn't the good friend I should have been. It was all wrong from before Day One and I don't know why. Did she resent me even back then because she'd done so much of the preparation? I thought the tension would go when we began walking. It didn't. It just became competitive and got worse. I've walked my journey, an all-consuming journey, and I wasn't prepared to let anything get in the way. Not friendship, not loneliness, not fear, not even at times my own body. For me, there wasn't another way, whatever the cost there was no alternative.

I wonder what she would write here, in the conclusion, the aftermath. What would be her truth?

When I sat down to write this I said to a friend something pretentious like:

"There's going to be two journeys—the physical one and the personal one" (man).

I got to the end and showed him the book.

"Where's the second journey?" he asked. "I thought you had a life-changing experience?"

And that made me pause. I mean, I haven't, essentially, changed. I don't think I've become more sympathetic and caring, just even more cautious about committing myself to an individual.

All that and there's been no journey? No 'moments of being'? No Wordsworthian flashes of enlightenment among the lupins? Can't possibly be true.

I've walked from Mexico to Canada. I've walked from one random line (border declared 1836) to another random line (border declared 1846). I've walked through Mojave, Kaweissu, Mono, Maidu, Shasta, Modoc, Klamath, Yakima, Clackamus, Snoquolmie, Skykomish, and so many more.

It wasn't until January that I saw the journey. The Bolivian Embassy hosted a talk/slideshow which I gave in London. They were grateful, overwhelmed.

"You did all that, walked all that way for Bolivia! It's wonderful."

And that touched me. I did all that for me, but also for people who will appreciate the help more than I can ever imagine. Everything you do or don't do has some kind of indirect or direct effect on someone else.

This one comment has changed me. Without the Amerindians there would be no Americans. Bizarre as that may sound, being as we practically wiped out the 600-odd nations of North America, it was they who fed and supported those first British settlements like Jamestown. The pilgrims aboard the Mayflower left Britain because of religious persecution. The majority of people on board however, were economic migrants, including one of my ancestors, John Carver of Doncaster. And when they got to America they were fed by the Amerindians. And then all those millions that followed over the centuries—what they could not get through generosity they took. So that's how I've changed. I am becoming political, motivated, idealistic.

And I do need my friends. Actually more than that, I no longer want to be self-sufficient. I want to live in London, see my friends often and maybe, maybe even fall in love. The next dream is waiting around the corner.

Of course, I've only been back a few months. It could all change again. We'll see.

> *There are many worlds. Some have passed and some are still to come. In one world the Indians all creep; in another they all walk; in another they all fly.*
> Pai Ute (near Kern River, California)[17]

Sometimes I think I crawled, other times that I walked, but occasionally at least, I know I flew.

ENDNOTES

[1] This book is now out of print. Please see Ray Jardine, *Beyond Backpacking*, (LaPine, 2000).

[2] **Hiker Update**: Bernard, the Lonely Wolf, only had a few weeks' holiday but did what he could to see the Californian countryside. He writes "I take twice a week massage session and do stretching in the gym to relax my crimpled body after so many years of splendid neglect," and is planning to hike again next summer.

[3] **Hiker Update**: I never did see them again, but heard the following: Kirk finished his hike in the Sierras as he missed his wife too much; Irish John bailed out at some point in California; Mike broke his leg and was air-lifted off Mt. Whitney; and Darris 'flip-flopped'—stopped at Cascade Summit, Oregon, got a lift north and then walked south from the border.

[4] **Hiker Update**: Mudflap and one of the Swiss guys left the trail from Anza. Matt the banker, I met again in Lone Pine, hitching his way around and taking brief trips into the mountains complete with fishing rod and mini guitar. He stopped there, having been offered a job too good to pass up. The second Swiss guy I never heard about again or saw in any of the registers, so presumably he went too. Doc Rudy went home for a week and then came back to finish the whole trail on 29th September.

[5] Gentle Ben Go, *Data Book,* (Sacramento, 1997).

[6] Quoted Tindal and Shi, *America: A Narrative History,* (New York and London, 1984).

[7] Frederick Russell Burnham, *Taking Chances,* (Los Angeles, 1944).

[8]   With thanks to Bob from Three Points Ranch who emailed to say it was him—thanks Bob!

[9]   John Muir, *Letter to a friend from Yosemite*, (29 May 1870).

[10] **Author's note**: Someone who read this book for me commented; "The Everybody-needs-a-Charles character disappears without comment, unforgivably if I may say so." Yes, well, I thought so too.

[11] **Hiker update:** Gene did make it to the end. He hit northern Washington in November (!) and made the decision to continue as long as he could see the trail, despite the fact that there was by then up to three feet of snow. Crazy. Arrived Manning Park on 14th November.

[12] John Muir, *Our National Parks,* (Boston and New York, 1901).

[13] As recorded by Katharine Berry Judson, *Myths and Legends of California and the Old Southwest,* (1912, Etext #2503).

[14] Taken from various sources.

[15] Ray Jardine, *The Pacific Crest Trail Hiker's Handbook,* (LaPine, 1996).

[16] **Hiker update:** Turtle and Lora got snowed off-trail about 50 miles from the border in mid-October. They finished their PCT hike in 2001.

[17] As recorded by Katharine Berry Judson, *Myths and Legends of California and the Old Southwest,* (1912, Pokoh, the Old Man).

Canada

Stehekin

Skykomish

Snoqualmie Pass

Washington

White Pass

Cascade Locks

Ollalie Lake

Oregon

Crater Lake

Seiad Valley

Burney Falls

Old Station

Belden

Sierra City

Echo Lake

Lone Pine

Kennedy Meadows

California

Mojave

Los Angeles

Agua Dulce

Warner Springs

Mexico

TABLES

Hiking Chart

Southern California

Date	Day	Destination	Miles Walked	Trail Miles North
30 Apr	1	Hauser Creek	16.7	15.7
1 May	2	Boulder Oak	10.4	26.1
2 May	3	Burnt Rancheria/*Mount Laguna	16.1	42.2
3 May	4	*Rest day*	1.4	
4 May	5	Pioneer Mail Trailhead	11.0	53.0
5 May	6	Rodriguez Spur	15.9	68.9
6 May	7	Scissors Crossing	9.2	78.1
7 May	8	W-W Ranch (turn-off)	15.6	91.7
8 May	9	San Ysidra Creek	14.1	105.8
9 May	10	*Warner Springs	9.4	112.4
10 May	11	dry river bed	2.0	112.9
11 May	12	Combs Peak	17.9	130.2
12 May	13	Tule Canyon Road/*Anza	9.4	138.3
13 May	14	*Rest day*		
14 May	15	*Rest day*		
15 May	16	*Rest day*		
16 May	17	*Rest day*		
17 May	18	Pines to Palms Highway/Anza	16.4	153.7
18 May	19	Cedar Spring (turn-off)	11.3	164.4
19 May	20	Red Tahquiz Mountain	13.4	176.8
20 May	21	San Jacinto River	9.4	186.4
21 May	22	Snow Creek	15.0	200.4
22 May	23	Pink Motel/*Cabazon	13.0	213.5
23 May	24	Teutang Canyon	4.9	218.4
24 May	25	Mission Creek	15.9	234.3
25 May	26	Coon Creek Jumpoff	13.8	248.1
26 May	27	Hollywood Mansion	15.9	264.0
27 May	28	Van Dusen Canyon/*Big Bear	12.3	276.3
28 May	29	Crab Flats Road	16.5	293.8
29 May	30	*Rest day*		
30 May	31	Deep Creek Hot Springs	15.4	309.2
31 May	32	Saddle, Silverwood Lake	18.5	326.9

1 Jun	33	Crowder Canyon	18.4	344.3
2 Jun	34	viewpoint on ridge-top	14.7	359.0
3 Jun	35	Grassy Hollows	13.9	372.9
4 Jun	36	Mount Williamson	17.6	389.7
5 Jun	37	Sulphur Springs	18.0	406.9
6 Jun	38	Big Buck Camp	19.6	426.3
7 Jun	39	Indian Canyon Road	17.8	444.1
8 Jun	40	*Agua Dulce	10.8	454.9
9 Jun	41	*Rest day*		
10 Jun	42	Green Valley Ranger Station	20.7	477.6
11 Jun	43	Sawmill Campground	19.0	496.6
12 Jun	44	*Highway 138/Jack Fair/Lancaster	19.4	516.0
13 Jun	45	Aqueduct	4.0	520.0
14 Jun	46	Tyler Horse Canyon +	21.0	541.0
15 Jun	47	Willow Springs Road/*Tehachapi	14.1	555.1
16 Jun	48	Waterfall Canyon	16.0	571.1
17 Jun	49	green gate	15.4	586.3
18 Jun	50	Cottonwood Creek	13.9	600.2
19 Jun	51	Pinyon Mountain	17.8	618.0
20 Jun	52	Forest	19.0	637.0
21 Jun	53	*Walker Pass/Onyx	11.4	647.8
22 Jun	54	*Rest day*		

Central California

Date	Day	Destination	Miles Walked	Trail Miles North
23 Jun	55	camp-spot	2.1	649.9
24 Jun	56	Joshua Tree Spring	13.6	659.3
25 Jun	57	Fox Mill Spring +	19.5	278.6
26 Jun	58	*Kennedy Meadows	20.2	698.8
27 Jun	59	Saddle Monache Creek Bowl	20.1	718.9
28 Jun	60	Mulkey Pass	19.7	738.2
29 Jun	61	Cottonwood Pass/*Lone Pine	8.6	743.8
30 Jun	62	*Rest day*		
1 Jul	63	*Rest day*		
2 Jul	64	*Rest day*		
3 Jul	65	Cottonwood Pass	3.0	
4 Jul	66	Guitar Lake	20.6	760.5
5 Jul	67	Crabtree Meadows	12.1	
6 Jul	68	Vidette Meadows	21.0	781.5
7 Jul	69	Lake Marjorie	23.3	803.8
8 Jul	70	Grouse Meadows	20.0	823.8
9 Jul	71	San Joaquin River	21.3	845.1
10 Jul	72	Hilgard Creek +	19.7	864.9

11 Jul	73	*Vermilion Valley	7.4	871.3
12 Jul	74	Lake Virginia	14.7	885.0
13 Jul	75	Minaret Falls	8.6	903.6
14 Jul	76	Marie Lakes	16.9	920.5
15 Jul	77	*Tuolumne Meadows	15.2	935.7
16 Jul	78	*Rest day*		
17 Jul	79	Miller Lake	18.7	954.4
18 Jul	80	Kerrick Canyon	19.0	973.4
19 Jul	81	Cascade Creek Footbridge	21.4	994.8
20 Jul	82	*Sonora Pass	18.4	1013.2
21 Jul	83	Saddle	18.2	1031.4
22 Jul	84	Pennsylvania Creek	20.4	1051.8
23 Jul	85	A sierra crest	20.4	1072.4
24 Jul	86	*Echo Lake	16.8	1089.2
25 Jul	87	Phipp's Creek	20.2	1109.4
26 Jul	88	Ward Peak	20.7	1130.1
27 Jul	89	Donner Pass/*Truckee	20.0	1150.1
28 Jul	90	*Rest day*		
29 Jul	91	Interstate 80	3.0	1153.1
30 Jul	92	Meadow Lake Road	15.8	1169.0
31 Jul	93	*Sierra City	23.5	1191.5
1 Aug	94	County-Line	22.7	1210.2
2 Aug	95	Logging Road	20.2	1230.4
3 Aug	96	ridge	21.0	1251.4
4 Aug	97	Clear Creek	22.7	1274.1
5 Aug	98	*Belden + 7miles	16.0	1290.1
6 Aug	99	Humboldt Summit +	20.0	1310.1
7 Aug	100	Stover Camp	22.8	1332.9
8 Aug	101	Grassy Swale	20.0	1350.9
9 Aug	102	*Old Station	22.3	1372.1
10 Aug	103	Hand-gliding knoll	22.0	1393.6
11 Aug	104	*Burney Falls	23.9	1417.5

Northern California and Oregon

Date	Day	Destination	Miles Walked	Trail Miles North
12 Aug	105	Peavine Creek	14.1	1431.6
13 Aug	106	6100 feet	20.0	1450.6
14 Aug	107	Ash Camp	19.3	1469.9
15 Aug	108	Riverside Road	29.8	1499.7
16 Aug	109	*Rest day*		
17 Aug	110	Gumboot Lake	25.7	1525.1

18 Aug	111	Kangaroo Lake	26.5	1550.3
19 Aug	112	Carter Meadows	30.9	1580.0
20 Aug	113	*Etna Summit	20.1	1600.2
21 Aug	114	Fisher Lake	14.1	1614.3
22 Aug	115	Black Mountain	11.7	1626.0
23 Aug	116	Cold Spring	18.1	1642.9
24 Aug	117	Grider Creek/*Seiad Valley	7.6	1650.5
25 Aug	118	Beardog Spring	19.5	1676.5
26 Aug	119	Sheep Camp Spring	21.6	1698.1
27 Aug	120	Callahans/*Ashland	23.4	1721.5
28 Aug	121	Major Int	2.7	1724.2
29 Aug	122	Hyatt Lake Resort	21.7	1745.1
30 Aug	123	South Branch Mt. Shelter	21.2	1765.5
31 Aug	124	Christi's Spring	22.9	1788.3
1 Sep	125	810	19.5	1809.6
2 Sep	126	*Mazama	15.7	1825.3
3 Sep	127	*Rest day*		
4 Sep	128	Crater Lake	3.0	1833.1
5 Sep	129	0.64	18.0	1865.4
6 Sep	130	Lake Pinewan	21.0	1886.4
7 Sep	131	Shelter Cove/*Crescent Lake	13.5	1907.1
8 Sep	132	Charlton lake	16.6	1925.3
9 Sep	133	Cliff Lake Shelter	19.0	1944.3
10 Sep	134	James Creek Shelter	23.2	1964.0
11 Sep	135	McKenzie Pass	19.5	1984.2
12 Sep	136	*Big Lake Youth Camp	11.4	1995.6
13 Sep	137	Rockpile Lake	19.9	2015.5
14 Sep	138	Scout Lake	19.3	2034.8
15 Sep	139	*Olallie Lake	13.1	2047.8
16 Sep	140	Warm Springs River	21.0	2068.7
17 Sep	141	broad saddle	25.6	2094.3
18 Sep	142	cluster	20.0	2113.1
19 Sep	143	7½ mile camp	22.5	2132.1
20 Sep	144	*Cascade Locks	7.5	2150.3

Washington

Date	Day	Destination	Miles Walked	Trail Miles North
21 Sep	145	Cedar Creek	8.6	2193.9
22 Sep	146	Cultus Creek Trail	21.0	2214.7
23 Sep	147	Swampy Creek	19.6	2234.3
24 Sep	148	"very good" campsite	18.9	2253.2

25 Sep	149	Rd 5603	3.4	2255.1
26 Sep	150	*Rest day*		
27 Sep	151	*Rest day*		
28 Sep	152	Two Lakes	20.9	2318.5
29 Sep	153	Chinook Pass/*Snoqualmie	9.0	2327.5
30 Sep	154	*Rest day*		
1 Oct	155	Park Lake	15.7	2412.3
2 Oct	156	Pete Lake	10.2	2418.0
3 Oct	157	Trailhead	4.0	
4 Oct	158	Snoqualmie		
5 Oct	159	Lake Valhalla	5.2	2477.1
6 Oct	160	Pass Creek	18.4	2495.5
7 Oct	161	Red Pass	14.8	2510.0
8 Oct	162	Mica Lake	17.2	2527.2
9 Oct	163	Suiattle River	15.7	2542.9
10 Oct	164	Five Mile Camp	21.4	2564.3
11 Oct	165	*Stehekin	5.1	2569.4
12 Oct	166	Rainy Pass	14.5	2589.1
13 Oct	167	Brush Creek	19.4	2607.5
14 Oct	168	Windy Pass	17.6	2624.8
15 Oct	169	Hopkins Lake	20.1	2644.7
16 Oct	170	Manning Park	14.2	2658.7